David Scott's Guide to
Investing in Mutual Funds

Other books on finance and investments
by David L. Scott

David Scott's Guide to Investing in Bonds
Dictionary of Accounting
Finance
Financing the Growth of Electric Utilities
Fundamentals of the Time Value of Money
The Guide to Buying Insurance
The Guide to Investing in Bonds
The Guide to Investing in Common Stocks
The Guide to Investing for Current Income
The Guide to Managing Credit
The Guide to Personal Budgeting
The Guide to Saving Money
The Guide to Tax-Saving Investing
How Stocks Work
How Wall Street Works
Investing in Tax-Saving Municipal Bonds
The Investor's Guide to Discount Brokers
Municipal Bonds: The Basics and Beyond
Security Investments
Stretching Your Income: 101 Ways to Fight Inflation
Understanding and Managing Investment Risk & Return
Wall Street Words

David Scott's Guide to Investing in Mutual Funds

David L. Scott

Professor of Accounting and Finance

Houghton Mifflin Company
Boston • New York

Visit our website: www.houghtonmifflinbooks.com

ISBN-13: 978-0-618-35328-6
ISBN-10: 0-618-35328-3

Library of Congress Cataloging-in-Publication Data
Scott, David Logan, 1942-
 [Guide to investing in mutual funds]
 David Scott's Guide to investing in mutual funds / David L. Scott.
   p. cm.
Edition for 1996 has title: The guide to investing in mutual funds.
c1996.
Includes index.
 ISBN 0-618-35328-3
 1. Mutual funds. I. Title: Guide to investing in mutual funds. II. Title.
HG4530.S39 2004
332.63'27--dc22

2003027521

Manufactured in the United States of America

Book design by Joyce C. Weston
Figure on p. 148 courtesy of Value Line Mutual Funds Survey; figure on p. 150 courtesy of Morningstar, Inc.

QWM 10 9 8 7 6 5 4 3 2 1

Contents

Introduction

Perhaps you are considering an investment in a mutual fund but hesitate because you don't fully understand how mutual funds use their shareholders' money to earn a return. You may consider a mutual fund to be a risky investment even though you aren't sure why. Perhaps you would like to buy shares of a mutual fund but are uncertain about what type of mutual fund it would be best to own. Maybe you have already invested in a mutual fund even though you didn't understand exactly what you were buying at the time. Perhaps you still don't. If you find yourself in any of these situations, or if you just plain don't understand what mutual funds do with their owners' money, this book is for you.

David Scott's Guide to Investing in Mutual Funds discusses the essentials of mutual funds for people who don't have much knowledge of these popular investments. The content of this book will help you to understand:

- how mutual funds are organized and brought to market;
- what kinds of income you can expect to earn if you invest in mutual funds;
- how to purchase and redeem mutual fund shares;
- the differences between equity funds, bond funds, and balanced funds;
- the importance of a mutual fund's investment objective;
- important considerations when selecting a mutual fund;

- how to save on fees that are levied on mutual fund investors;
- alternative investments to mutual funds;
- where to search for unbiased information about mutual funds.

Mutual funds are not particularly difficult to understand, especially when you have some knowledge about the common stocks and bonds that these investment companies own. Those of you who need to brush up a little on these securities will find basic information on stocks and bonds in Chapters 3 and 4. The better you understand these investments, the more likely you are to choose a fund that best serves your investment needs.

To make a wise investment in a mutual fund, you need to know more than just where to send your check. Mutual funds are offered in many varieties, from the ultra safe to the very risky. The shares of some mutual funds are subject to wide fluctuations in value, which can cause you to suffer substantial losses, especially if you must sell your shares on relatively short notice. Other mutual funds virtually guarantee that you can sell your shares for the price you paid.

You may feel the professional managers employed by a mutual fund should be able to solve most of your investment problems. After all, how can you go wrong when well-paid, high-powered financial advisers are managing the mutual fund's investments? Shouldn't you be able to rely on the financial managers to take care of investing your money to maximum advantage? In truth, even a well-managed mutual fund may turn out to be a poor investment choice if the fund's investment objective is not consistent with your own investment goals.

David L. Scott
Valdosta, Georgia

1 An Introduction to Mutual Funds

A mutual fund is a financial organization that utilizes the money invested by its shareholders to acquire a portfolio of securities that is managed for the benefit of the owners. Mutual funds enjoy a unique corporate structure that permits its stockholders to redeem their shares at any time directly through the company or its agents. Shareholders of a mutual fund earn a return from dividends and realized capital gains that are earned and distributed by the fund, and from possible increases in the market value of the shares they own. Mutual funds are attractive investment alternatives for individuals who desire access to diversified and professionally managed portfolios of securities.

Mutual funds have become one of America's favorite investments. From a mid-1920s introduction in the United States, the mutual fund industry has expanded until in early 2003 there were over 8,000 different funds holding net assets valued at more than $6.3 trillion. Whether you are interested in investing money in bonds, stocks, or a combination of the two, you may be able to invest more profitably and with less risk by choosing mutual funds rather than individual issues of common stocks and bonds.

Thousands of mutual funds offer virtually any type of diversi-

> **Tip** Mutual funds offer an easy and inexpensive investment vehicle for individuals to acquire a diversified stock or bond portfolio. However, keep in mind that the extent of diversification varies from fund to fund. Some funds are very diversified while other funds concentrate their investments in a specific industry.

fied or specialized stock or bond portfolio you desire. Many mutual funds specialize in owning the common stocks of growth companies while other mutual funds invest primarily in stocks that offer a high return from dividend payments. An increasing number of mutual funds have a narrow focus and concentrate on owning the stocks of companies that operate in a specific industry or companies that focus their operations in particular countries or regions of the world. Still other mutual funds invest only in specific types of fixed-income debt such as bonds that have long maturities, risky bonds that offer unusually high yields, or bonds that pay tax-exempt interest. Some mutual funds even restrict their investments to tax-exempt bonds that have been issued in a particular state. Figure 1 illustrates the spectacular growth in the number of mutual funds offered to investors. Notice that growth tapered off and the number of funds actually began to decline slightly with the beginning of the bear market that started near the turn of the century. Rising markets attract investors while falling markets cause individuals to search for more secure investments.

The Fundamentals of Mutual Funds

A mutual fund is a special type of investment company that invests its owners' money in financial assets such as stocks and bonds. Manufacturing and service companies—such as

Figure 1 ■ Growth in the Number of Mutual Funds, 1980–2002

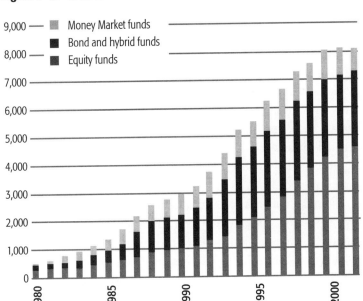

ConocoPhillips, Coca-Cola, General Electric, and Apple Computer—use the capital contributed by their owners and creditors to pay for equipment, land, buildings, and production materials used to produce goods or services that are sold to earn a profit for the owners. Rather than purchase assets that can be used to manufacture things or do things, mutual funds use stockholder capital to buy stocks, bonds, and money market securities for the benefit of the funds' owners. And while most companies serve customers who are distinct from the firms' shareholders (for example, General Motors sells vehicles to individuals and companies), a mutual fund has no customers other than the owners who have invested their savings in shares of the fund. You can only benefit from the services of a mutual fund if you become a shareholder of the fund.

The Organizational Structure of a Mutual Fund

A special corporate structure allows a mutual fund to stand ready to continuously sell shares of ownership, both to new investors and to existing shareholders, and to redeem outstanding shares of ownership. Thus, investors can purchase shares of a mutual fund at the same time that other shareholders "cash out," or have their shares redeemed. A mutual fund may occasionally halt the sale of shares to new investors, but these "closed" funds are a rarity. Mutual funds can grow larger and larger so long as investors continue to purchase additional shares of stock.

A typical corporation infrequently issues new shares of its own stock. A company may issue shares of stock in an initial public offering and not sell additional shares for many years. Established corporations that retain much of their profits for reinvestment in new assets may not sell additional shares for decades. Likewise, most corporations repurchase their shares of stock only occasionally or not at all, causing shareholders who wish to sell their shares to seek other investors who are interested in buying them. A shareholder who wishes to sell shares of stock must normally use the services of a brokerage firm that has access to securities markets where orders are entered by other investors.

A mutual fund's ability to sell additional shares of its own stock and to redeem its outstanding shares on demand stems both from the fund's corporate structure and from the nature of the assets it holds. Many stocks and bonds are actively traded, which allows mutual fund portfolio managers to easily invest additional money and to sell stocks and bonds from the firm's portfolio. Additional bonds and shares of stock are acquired when a mutual fund takes in more money from shares it issues than it pays out for shares that it redeems. Securities often have to be sold from a mutual fund's portfolio when the fund's shareholders redeem more shares than other investors purchase. Fund managers should not have difficulty increasing or decreasing the size of the fund's portfolio so long as an active market exists in the securities a mutual fund owns.

The typical manufacturing or service company owns many assets that would be difficult to sell on short notice. These companies could not operate effectively if the managers knew they might be required to sell some of the assets whenever their shareholders decided to redeem shares. Likewise, most companies (other than mutual funds) are unable to acquire additional assets whenever investors decide they would like to purchase more shares of stock.

Mutual Fund Decision Making

Directors elected by a mutual fund's stockholders are responsible for hiring managers who oversee day-to-day operations of the fund. The directors are also responsible for making certain that the managers pursue the fund's stated investment objectives. The fund covers its expenses, including the managers' compensation, from fees that are based on the amount of assets that are managed. Successful portfolio managers (i.e., those who profitably invest shareholders' funds) will attract additional investors to buy shares in the fund, thereby increasing both the size of the fund and the income earned by the fund and its managers. The more money the managers of a mutual fund are able to earn for the shareholders, the more money the managers will earn for themselves and their fund.

The directors of a mutual fund must select a *transfer agent* that will maintain shareholder records, issue new shares of stock, redeem outstanding shares of stock, and make payments to the fund's shareholders. The mutual fund must employ the services of a *custodian bank* or *trust company* to safeguard the fund's assets, make payments for securities purchases, and take charge of proceeds from the sale of securities. A single bank frequently serves both as custodian and transfer agent.

Investing in a mutual fund means you hitch your financial wagon to the decisions of the fund's portfolio managers. The better the investment decisions that are made by a mutual fund's investment managers, the larger the return you will earn on your investment in the fund. Your shares will increase in value if the investment managers select stocks and bonds that rise in value. On the other hand, your shares will decline, or increase less than you expected, if a mutual fund's managers make poor investment decisions.

In summary, a mutual fund:

1. pools your funds with money contributed by hundreds or thousands of other investors who have similar investment goals;

2. invests the shareholders' pooled monies in securities that are consistent with the fund's stated investment objectives;

3. provides for professional management of the fund's financial resources; and

4. pays dividends and distributes capital gains from income earned by the fund.

Why Mutual Funds Are Popular Investments

Several reasons help explain the tremendous increase in both the number of mutual funds and the amount of assets that these investment companies manage. Many individuals became acquainted with mutual funds in the mid and late 1970s, when market interest rates were high relative to the interest rates that federal regulation permitted banks and savings and loan associations to pay on insured savings accounts. The comparatively low returns available on savings accounts caused individuals to move billions of dollars from depository financial institutions to specialized mutual funds that offered liquidity, safety, and relatively high yields. Investments in these narrowly focused funds opened the floodgates to subsequent investments in equity (i.e., stock) and bond funds offered by many of the same fund sponsors. The tremendous increase in mutual fund shareholder accounts spurred by the bull markets of the 1980s and 1990s is illustrated in Figure 2.

Mutual funds that invest in stocks and bonds also benefited from increases in the market prices of securities during the 1980s and 1990s. Strong markets for stocks and bonds attracted new investors who saw an opportunity to earn returns that were substantially higher than the returns being earned on

Figure 2 ■ Mutual Fund Shareholder Accounts, 1980–2001

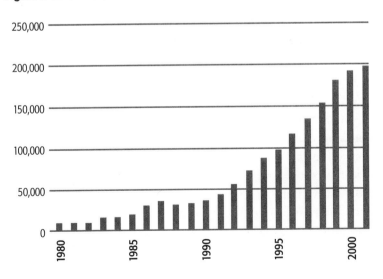

their existing investments. While many individuals invested directly in stocks and bonds, others chose to entrust their savings to the mutual funds that owned these investments. The high returns also encouraged individuals who already held mutual fund shares to invest additional money.

On an individual basis, mutual fund investments allow you to buy a single asset (i.e., shares of a mutual fund) and enjoy the benefit of an investment that is comprised of many different stocks and/or bonds. With only a relatively small amount of money, you can achieve instant diversification by investing in a mutual fund. Mutual funds have attracted many investors who feel more comfortable having their money managed by professional money managers than they do investing on their own. The need for professional management is especially important as the markets have become more volatile and new and complicated investment products have been introduced.

The Advantages of Professional Investment Management

Individuals often find it difficult to make investment decisions that involve common stocks and bonds. If you are like most individual investors, your waking hours are consumed by short periods of relaxation sandwiched around your job, family responsibilities, and meetings of professional, charitable, and social organizations. You probably don't have enough free hours to study annual reports, read financial newsletters, and review brokerage house recommendations. Even professionals employed in the financial services industry often choose to have their personal funds managed by other professionals.

Without time to stay current on the investment scene, how can you possibly compete with other investors, especially professional money managers whose full-time job is to seek out undervalued stocks and bonds? Even when you are able to carve out some extra time to read financial reports, you are likely to have difficulty interpreting all of the gobbledygook that fills most of them. You may be unsure about which securities to purchase, what price you should pay, and how long you should hold on to an investment. Should you adopt a buy-and-hold strategy in which you try to make certain you purchase the "right" stocks or bonds with the intention of holding these securities through thick and thin, or should you actively trade securities, moving your money from one security to another as you determine that some security prices are too low and others are too high? If you choose the latter course, how do you determine which securities to sell and when to sell them?

Rather than struggle with the many investment decisions that you should address when you purchase individual securities issues, you may be one of the many investors who decide to invest in shares of mutual funds and to trust the judgment of professional investment managers who are paid to supervise portfolios of securities. Mutual fund portfolio managers decide which securities to buy, how long to hold them, and which securities to replace them with. The managers decide when to adopt a conservative investment stance and when to invest more aggressively. The availability of professional investment managers means that, as an individual investor, you are required only to determine which managers to employ (i.e., what fund to invest in) and when you make your investments. Subsequent chapters in this book discuss the wide variety of mutual funds that are available for purchase and how you can go about choosing among all these funds.

The Importance of Diversification

A major advantage of investing in mutual funds is the substantial diversification that can be achieved with a relatively small investment. When you purchase mutual fund shares, your investment is immediately spread among the many individual securities that are owned by the fund, a degree of diversification that would be impossible if you attempted to assemble a portfolio of your own. At any particular time a mutual fund typically owns a hundred or more different securities; this provides substantial protection against major losses caused by declines in individual issues. For example, unfavorable news about a particular company or industry may have a negative effect on the market value of a mutual fund's portfolio, but the overall impact will be mitigated because the mutual fund's portfolio contains such a large number of securities, most of which remain unaffected by the news. Diversification does not eliminate all risk, of course, but it does reduce the risk you would face by owning shares of stock in two, three, or four companies.

Most individual investors who purchase individual stock and bond issues are unable to achieve effective diversification unless they invest only small amounts of money in individual securities. For example, with $10,000 to invest you will have to limit your investments to a relatively small sum in each security in order to achieve even minimal diversification. Small investments tend to result in relatively large commissions and cause added headaches as you maintain a record of many different purchases, sales, and dividend payments.

Tip Diversification is important but it doesn't mean you need to invest in a large number of mutual funds. Proper selection of a limited number of funds can provide all of the diversification you require. Too many mutual funds will complicate your life with additional mail and paperwork.

All mutual funds are not equally diversified. Many funds intentionally limit their diversification efforts and concentrate on investments in a specific industry or in companies that operate in a particular geographic region of the world. Likewise, many mutual funds limit their investments to common stocks while other funds invest only in bonds. Specialized mutual funds offer much less diversification and subject their shareholders to much more risk compared to mutual funds that invest in many different and diverse industries. Investing in the shares of specialized mutual funds results in a much greater likelihood that you will incur large financial losses (or large financial gains) compared to investors who choose diversified funds.

The Ability to Shift Investments at Low Cost

Some mutual fund sponsors direct many different funds that have a wide range of investment objectives. For example, a single company may sponsor separate mutual funds that invest in money market securities, speculative stocks, high-grade bonds, tax-exempt securities, and junk bonds. Some sponsors oversee several different funds with similar investment objectives. Sponsors of these families of funds generally permit shareholders of one fund to transfer their investment to one or more of the other funds for a nominal fee. Suppose you have invested in the shares of a mutual fund specializing in growth stocks and the fund is part of a family of funds. If you expect the stock market to decline during the next six months, shares of your stock fund could be redeemed and the proceeds reinvested in the shares of a money market fund or a short-term bond fund operated by the same sponsor. Some of the larger mutual fund distributors are listed in Figure 3 (p. 12).

Choosing to invest in individual securities (as opposed to mutual funds) can result in substantial brokerage fees if you

Figure 3 ■ A Select List of Large Mutual Fund Distributors

AIM Fund Services, Inc.
PO box 4739
Houston, TX 77210
800-959-4246
www.aiminvestments.com

Alliance Global Investor Services, Inc.
PO Box 746003
San Antonio, TX 78278
800-251-0539
www.alliancecapital.com

Eaton Vance Mutual Funds
PO Box 9653
Providence, RI 02940
800-262-1122
www.eatonvance.com

Fidelity Investments
PO Box 770001
Cincinnati, OH 45277
800-343-3543
www.fidelity.com

Janus
PO Box 173375
Denver, CO 80217
800-525-3713
www.janus.com

MFS Fund Distributors, Inc.
500 Boylston Street
Boston, MA 02116
800-225-2606
www.mfs.com

Nuveen Investor Services
PO Box 8530
Boston, MA 02266
800-257-8787
www.nuveen.com

Oppenheimer Funds
PO Box 5270
Denver, CO 80217
800-525-7048
www.oppenheimerfunds.com

Putnam Investor Services
PO Box 41203
Providence, RI 02940
800-225-1581
www.putnaminvestments.com/individual

Scudder Investments Service Company
PO Box 219151
Kansas City, MO 64121
800-621-1048
www.scudder.com

Strong Investments
P.O. Box 2936
Milwaukee, WI 53201
800-359-3379
www.estrong.com

T. Rowe Price
P.O. Box 17630
Baltimore, MD 21297
800-225-5132
www.troweprice.com

The Vanguard Group
PO Box 1110
Valley Forge, PA 19480
877-662-7447
flagship4.vanguard.com

conduct business through a full-service brokerage firm. If you sell most or all of your shares of stock in order to move the money into intermediate-term bonds, you pay a commission to sell the stock, an additional commission to purchase the bonds, and yet another commission if you later decide to move the money back to the stock market. The emergence of online brokerage firms with their low commissions has reduced the cost of investing for investors who purchase individual stocks and bonds. However, even these firms generally impose relatively high fees for small trades.

The Nominal Investment Requirement

Mutual funds have established minimums for initial investments and for subsequent purchases of additional shares. Funds typically require an initial investment of from $250 to $2,500 (depending upon the fund) to establish an account, although some mutual funds have minimums of $10,000 and more. Some funds allow additional share purchases with as little as $50 once an account has been established. Each fund's sponsor establishes the fund's minimum investment requirement.

Mutual Fund Services

Competition for investors has caused mutual funds to offer their shareholders a variety of useful services, often at no additional cost (although additional services that cost the sponsor money may ultimately reduce the returns earned by shareholders). The availability and details of each fund's services are spelled out in the free prospectus that you should study prior to investing your money. The relative value of each service depends upon your investment needs. You may have little need for a specific service that other investors might consider nearly indispensable. Some of the more popular services offered by mutual funds include the following:

Check-writing privileges Most money market funds and many bond funds permit shareholders to write checks on their accounts. Funds that offer check writing generally establish a minimum amount (typically $500 or $1,000) for which a check can be written, and a few funds charge a nominal fee for each check written. Some funds establish a limit on the number of checks that can be written each month. Although these accounts are not a viable substitute for a bank checking account, check writing is the ultimate method for redeeming your shares in a mutual fund. Rather than request that the fund redeem shares and send you a check in the mail, you merely write a check to pay for something or make a deposit in your bank account. The check is processed through the Federal Reserve check-clearing system and presented for payment to your mutual fund's transfer agent, which will redeem the appropriate number of shares required to cover the check. Your investment in the mutual fund continues to earn interest until the check is presented for payment.

Automatic investing Many funds allow customers to arrange for a regular transfer of money from a bank account to the fund in order to purchase shares of the fund. Some mutual fund distributors permit individuals to acquire shares through automatic payroll deductions from their paychecks. Automatic investing is a good way to implement a dollar-cost averaging system like that discussed in Chapter 7.

Reinvestment of dividends and capital gains distributions Shareholders generally have an option to reinvest dividends and capital gains distributions into additional shares of stock of the fund. Choosing the reinvestment option is similar to reinvesting interest from a savings account; both actions will cause the value of your account to grow more rapidly. Reinvestment is practical only when you do not require current investment income to meet living expenses. Many mutual fund investors choose to receive dividends and reinvest capital gains distributions.

Wire transfers Wire transfers of money are permitted by many mutual funds. A wire transfer allows you to rapidly transfer money to or from a mutual fund. For example, you can request that shares be sold and the proceeds wired to your bank account or brokerage account so that you have instant access to the funds. You will be required to request wire transfer privileges before you are able to access this service, and a nominal fee is likely to be charged for each wire transfer that is initiated.

Switching Also called *exchanging*, switching is a handy means for moving all or a portion of your money out of one mutual fund and into the shares of another mutual fund operated by the same company. Switching among funds was mentioned briefly in the earlier discussion of families of funds. Suppose you invested all your money in a mutual fund that holds a portfolio of long-term corporate bonds but have now decided that you would like to move a portion of your money into growth stocks. If you have invested with a mutual fund sponsor that operates several funds with different investment objectives, you may be able to switch your investment from the bond fund to a growth

Tip Many mutual fund investors choose to reinvest dividend and capital gains distributions. Be certain before you sign up for a reinvestment plan that you will not be charged a sales fee for shares that are purchased in this manner.

stock fund with no more than a small fee. Mutual fund sponsors that offer exchange privileges generally require transfers of a minimum size and sometimes establish restrictions on the number of exchanges you can make during a given period of time. In addition, some funds levy a penalty in the event you don't hold shares for a specified period.

Retirement accounts Retirement accounts are a popular offering of nearly all mutual funds, which have become one of the major players in the market for Individual Retirement Accounts (IRAs), self-employed retirement plans (Keogh plans), corporate retirement plans (401k plans), and rollovers from existing IRAs or pension plans. Opening a retirement account at a mutual fund often provides access to investment vehicles with a wide variety of investment objectives. Mutual funds have varying charges for establishing and servicing different types of retirement plans.

Regulation of Mutual Funds

Mutual funds are subject to substantial regulation at several levels. The initial regulation affecting investment companies that was passed during the 1930s was occasioned by excesses in the industry prior to the Great Crash of 1929. Mutual fund regulation is primarily designed to make certain that the funds operate in a responsible manner and that investors have the opportunity to learn about the fees, investment policies, and past performance of a particular mutual fund. Neither federal nor state regulation ensures that a mutual fund's advisers will render good investment advice or that your investment in a fund's shares will prove profitable.

At the federal level the Securities Act of 1933, also called the "Truth in Securities Act," requires all issuers of new securities and some secondary offerings, including mutual funds, to file with the federal government a registration statement that provides extensive details about the company. The act also requires that a mutual fund provide investors with a current prospectus describing the fund's policies and investment objectives. The primary purpose of this act is to make certain that companies issuing securities provide full disclosure of relevant information so that investors have the opportunity to make informed investment decisions.

The following year Congress passed the Securities Exchange Act of 1934 that established the Securities and Exchange Commission (SEC) and vested the organization with a variety of enforcement powers. The 1934 act extended disclosure requirements to securities that are traded in the secondary market (e.g., the over-the-counter market and organized exchanges such as the New York Stock Exchange). Mutual fund distributors are subject to regulation by the National Association of Securities Dealers (NASD) and the Securities and Exchange Commission.

The Investment Company Act of 1940 is one of the major pieces of legislation providing for the federal regulation of mutual funds. The 1940 act requires mutual funds to (1) provide investors with accurate information, (2) guarantee that shareholders will have a say in certain matters affecting the funds, (3) use approved accounting methods, (4) maintain adequate liquidity, (5) operate in the interest of shareholders, and (6) refrain from levying excessive fees and charges. Separate legislation produced the Investment Advisors Act of 1940, which regulates the activities of mutual fund advisers.

The Investment Company Amendments Act of 1970 imposes a fiduciary standard on the managers, officers, and directors of an investment company. The act also facilitates a shareholder protest of sales charges and other expenses.

Mutual funds are also subject to regulation by the states in which they are organized and the states in which shares are distributed to investors. Individuals who distribute mutual fund shares are subject to federal and state regulation. Having all these regulations in place gives some protection against deceptive or fraudulent practices. It does not mean that you will not lose money from your mutual fund investments.

Income and Taxation

The bottom line to any investment is the after-tax return you earn. Earnings from an investment must be considered in light of the taxes you will be required to pay on the income received. Mutual funds can potentially produce three types of income for shareholders. In most instances this income is taxable to the shareholders but not to the mutual funds.

Sources of Income for Mutual Fund Shareholders

Mutual fund shareholders have three possible sources of income:

1. Dividends that the mutual fund pays to its shareholders from the dividend and interest income earned from securities

> **Tip**
>
> Small mutual funds tend to enjoy the investment flexibility of being able to take investment positions in relatively small companies. Large mutual funds have less flexibility in that they must normally restrict their investments to the securities of big companies with many outstanding shares.

held in the fund's portfolio. A mutual fund will receive dividends from stocks and interest from bonds that it owns. Virtually all of this dividend and interest income is passed through to the mutual fund's shareholders as dividend payments. Dividends may be paid monthly or quarterly depending on the fund.

2. Capital gains distributions to stockholders when securities owned by the mutual fund are sold at a gain. For example, if a mutual fund purchases 50,000 shares of Coca-Cola common stock for $38 per share and subsequently sells the stock for $48 per share, the fund realizes a capital gain of $500,000 (50,000 shares at a gain of $10 per share) that can be distributed to the fund's shareholders. Capital gains distributions are generally made annually near the end of the calendar year.

3. Increases in the value of the mutual fund's shares that result from increases in the value of securities owned by the fund. If the mutual fund invests in securities that subsequently increase in value, the value of the mutual fund's shares will also increase. In the previous example, the mutual fund's shares would have a greater value if the fund's managers decided to retain rather than sell the Coca-Cola stock.

Taxation of Mutual Fund Income

A mutual fund that meets Internal Revenue Service requirements to qualify as a regulated investment company is not required to pay taxes on the dividends, interest, and capital gains the fund earns. Regulated investment companies are nothing but conduits that pass income along to their shareholders who are required to pay taxes on the income at rates based on their personal taxable income. To qualify as a regulated investment company, a mutual fund must comply with certain regulations regarding asset diversification and must distribute at least 90 percent of its taxable income to shareholders.

In general, ordinary income earned by a mutual fund is taxed as ordinary income to the shareholders while capital gains earned by a fund are taxed as capital gains to the shareholders. For example, if your income is taxed at a marginal rate of 27 percent, dividend distributions received from a mutual fund will be taxed at a rate of 27 percent. Individuals with substantial taxable income who may be in a higher tax bracket will be taxed on mutual fund dividend distributions at a higher rate. Mutual fund distributions of income not normally taxable to individuals (e.g., interest received from municipal bonds) remain nontaxable when received by shareholders. You must report and pay taxes on mutual fund dividend distributions even if you have chosen to have your distributions automatically reinvested in additional shares of the mutual fund.

> **Tip** Mutual funds offer an efficient method for investing in foreign companies with securities that trade in overseas markets. Foreign companies often disclose minimal financial information, thereby making it difficult to evaluate their securities.

A gain in the market value of a mutual fund's shares is not taxable until the shares are sold and the gain is realized. The difference between the price paid to purchase the shares (your "basis") and the price received from the sale of the shares (the "net proceeds") determines the amount of income that is subject to taxation. You will not be taxed on gains so long as you continue to hold mutual fund shares. Unrealized gains are sometimes called "paper gains," because the increase is on paper rather than realized as cash. Likewise, losses in value cannot be used to reduce taxable income until the shares are sold and a loss is realized.

At the end of each year, mutual funds are required to send each shareholder a form that lists the types and amounts of distributions made to stockholders. Information on distributions to individual shareholders is also forwarded to the Internal Revenue Service, which utilizes the data to check the accuracy of the information on your tax return.

Determining the Cost Basis of Shares that Are Sold

When shares of a mutual fund are sold you will need to compute the gain or loss that must be reported to the Internal Revenue Service on Schedule D of your federal tax return. Calculating a gain or loss requires that you determine the cost, or basis, of the shares that have been sold. The amount of the gain or loss is determined by subtracting the cost from the price you receive when the shares are sold. Many investors find it confusing to determine which particular shares have been sold.

The gain or loss is easy to calculate when all of your shares have been purchased at the same price. Suppose you purchase 1,000 shares at a price of $15.20 and later sell half these shares at a price of $20.00 each. You decide to retain the other 500 shares. Your gain is $4.80 per share ($20.00 sale price less your cost of $15.20) times the 500 shares sold, or $2,400. This is the realized gain that must be reported to the Internal Revenue Service. The $15.20 cost basis of the remaining shares will be utilized to calculate the gain or loss when the shares are sold at some later date.

If all the shares sold in a transaction have been acquired at many different prices, as would be the case if you chose to reinvest dividend and capital gains distributions, the calculation of gains and losses is somewhat more complicated because many different costs bases come into play. Still, there will be a record of the prices you paid, so you shouldn't have great difficulty in calculating gains or losses. Now suppose you acquired shares in a fund on several dates at different prices. Perhaps you purchased 100 shares at a price of $14.00 per share and acquired an additional 4 shares at $14.50 per share and yet another 5 shares at $15.00 per share. If you sell all the shares at a price of $17.00, your total gain will be $300 + $10 + $10, or $320. Another method of arriving at the same gain is to calculate the weighted average price you paid for the shares and then subtract the answer from the price at which your shares have been sold. You then multiply the difference between the sale price and the average cost by the number of shares sold.

Selling a portion of the shares you have acquired at several different prices presents a challenge in determining gains or losses. Suppose you originally purchased 600 shares at a price of $15.20, and later you purchased an additional 400 shares at varying prices over the course of many years. Now, when you sell 500 mutual fund shares, which shares are you selling and which shares are you keeping? The answer is important because it will determine the cost basis that is used to calculate the gain. Are all 500 shares sold the original shares, or are you selling 100 of the original shares and 400 shares acquired through reinvestment? Determining which shares you sold may seem a pointless exercise, but you must know which shares are sold in order to arrive at a cost basis that is used to calculate your realized gain and tax liability. Several acceptable methods are available for determining the cost basis of mutual fund shares that are sold. These are:

First acquired, first sold Unless otherwise indicated, the Internal Revenue Service assumes that the first shares acquired are the first shares sold. This method assumes that you have sold 500 of your 600 original shares. In the above example this method would produce a basis of $15.20 per share for calculating the gain because these were the first 500 shares acquired.

Average cost In this method, you divide the total amount you have invested in all the shares you currently own by the number of shares of the mutual fund you currently own to determine the average cost of the shares. The gain per share is calculated by subtracting the average cost from the sale price.

Specific shares In this method, you instruct the mutual fund to sell shares that you acquired on specific dates and use the cost of these shares for the cost basis in calculating the size of your gain or loss. A reported gain and immediate tax liability are minimized if you direct the fund to sell shares that have been purchased at the highest price. Keep in mind that reducing your immediate tax liability by assuming shares with the highest cost are sold will increase your future tax liability. This may or may not be a good idea. Figure 4 (pp. 24–25) provides an example of each of the three methods of calculating the basis for the sale of mutual fund shares.

Figure 4 ■ Determining Gains and Losses from the Sale of Mutual Fund Shares

Suppose you purchase shares in the Vandewalker Growth Fund over a period of several years. The record of your purchases is as follows:

Date Purchased	Amount Invested	Price	Shares Bought	Shares Owned
03/07/01	$5,000.00	$16.00	333.333	333.333
06/15/02	3,000.00	14.50	206.897	540.230
08/20/02	2,500.00	15.10	165.563	705.793
11/10/02	2,800.00	15.30	183.007	888.800
12/15/02*	844.36	16.25	51.961	940.761
02/09/03	2,000.00	16.12	124.069	1,064.830
06/28/03	2,500.00	15.75	158.730	1,223.560
07/10/03	600.00	16.50	36.364	1,259.924
10/12/03	3,000.00	16.75	179.104	1,439.028

* reinvestment of 95 cents per share distribution

The total amount invested is $22,244.36
The average cost per share is $15.45 ($22,244.36/1,439.028 shares)

A. Suppose on 12/01/03 you sell all the shares at the current price of $17.00 per share. Your total gain equals the gain per share ($17.00 minus $15.45, or $1.55) times the number of shares you sell (1,439.028), or $2,230.49. Gains from the sale of shares that have been held over one year (888.800 shares x $1.55, or $1,377.64) qualify as long-term. The remaining portion of the gain is classified as short-term.

   An alternative method is to compute the average cost for shares held over a year and use this cost to determine your long-term gain, and to compute the average cost for shares held a year or less and use this cost to determine your short-term gain.

B. Suppose on 12/01/03 you sell 800 shares at the current price of $17.00 per share. The remaining 639.028 shares continue to be held in your account.

The three methods for determining your cost basis result in the following gains, one of which must be used to calculate your tax liability.

1. *Average price:* The total gain equals the sale price minus the average cost ($17.00 – $15.45, or $1.55) times the number of shares sold (800), or $1,240.00.

2. *First bought, first sold:* Calculate the gain for each group of shares to a total of 800 shares, beginning with the first shares purchased. Using information provided in the purchase record, you have a gain of $2.00 per share ($17.00 – $15.00) on the first 333.333 shares, $2.50 per share ($17.00 – $14.50) on the next 206.897 shares, $1.90 ($17.00 – $15.10) on the next 165.563 shares, and $1.70 ($17.00 – $15.30) on 94.207 of the 183.007 shares purchased on 11/10/02. The total gain of $1,658.63 is classified as long-term because all of the shares sold have been held over a year.

3. *Selected shares:* To minimize the gain reported to tax authorities you should request that the mutual fund sell shares purchased at the highest prices. If minimizing your gain is the goal request that the fund sell 179.104 shares bought at $16.75, 36.364 shares bought at $16.50, 51.961 shares purchased for $16.25, 124.069 shares bought at $16.12, 158.730 shares purchased at $15.75, 183.007 shares bought for $15.30 each, and 66.765 of the 165.563 shares bought at $15.10. The total gain using this approach is $852.49.

Several considerations should influence your choice of a method for allocating the cost for shares that are sold. First, take account of which shares have been owned for over a year and qualify as long-term holdings. In this case, shares purchased prior to 12/01/02 would be considered long-term holdings and qualify for special tax consideration. Even though these shares tend to have a lower cost and will result in a larger gain, you may benefit from the lower tax rate that is likely to apply. Second, if you believe tax rates are likely to increase in the future, you may wish to direct the fund to sell shares with the lowest cost in order to take advantage of today's lower tax rates. The world of taxation is one of endless complication.

2 The Operation and Valuation of a Mutual Fund

The value of a share in a mutual fund is determined by dividing the total market value of the fund's securities portfolio (less any debts) by the number of outstanding shares of the mutual fund's stock. The share value determines the price shareholders will receive for shares that are redeemed and the price investors will pay for new shares. The total market value of a mutual fund's portfolio expands and contracts as investors purchase and redeem the fund's shares. The redemption of outstanding shares and sale of new shares have little effect on shareholders who continue to hold their shares.

Chapter 1 explained that mutual funds are structured in an unusual fashion compared to other corporations. A mutual fund continuously offers new shares of stock for sale at the same time the fund stands ready to redeem its outstanding shares. Mutual funds enjoy this flexibility to continuously issue and redeem shares because of the great liquidity of the assets they hold. The continuous and active market in most stock and bond issues permits a mutual fund's managers to readily invest new money and to quickly sell securities from the fund's portfolio.

Depending upon whether investors are, on balance, buying new shares or redeeming outstanding shares of a particular mutual fund, the total value of the fund's portfolio (but not necessarily per-share value) will expand or contract. Management that has demonstrated that it is adept at identifying securities that appreciate in value will attract new investors at the same time current shareholders are likely to increase their investment in the fund. In other words, a successful fund will issue additional shares and grow larger. A mutual fund that issues many additional shares will swell in size and require the fund's portfolio managers to invest substantial amounts of new money. Investment managers who do a poor job of selecting securities are likely to cause investor redemptions that exceed the sale of new shares, resulting in a reduction in the fund's size. The linkage is clear: In the mutual fund business, the good get bigger and the bad get smaller. Several years of superior investment performance can cause a mutual fund to grow to many times its previous size.

The best way to explain the organization and operation of a mutual fund is to take a step-by-step journey beginning at the time a fund is conceived and carrying through to a point when investment managers begin making changes to the composition of the portfolio.

Establishing the Grits Fund

Suppose you and a group of semi-wealthy associates decide to pool your investment capital and establish an investment com-

| Tip | The sponsor of a mutual fund may decide to close the fund to new investors in order to keep the assets under management from growing too large to effectively manage. Mutual funds with a successful track record attract new investors and often grow to such a large size that investment flexibility is hindered. |

pany called the Grits Fund. Members of the group have job and family responsibilities that have caused them to grow weary of managing their investments on an individual basis. You and your associates have spent many hours discussing the generally poor investment advice you receive and the losses you have suffered on your investments. You have finally concluded that a collective effort should produce improved investment results.

Investing as a group should produce savings on brokerage commissions because of the smaller proportional fees charged by brokerage firms for stock transactions that involve more shares. More importantly, you expect improved investment performance because your group is planning to enlist the services of an experienced money manager who will select and manage a portfolio of securities for your benefit. You feel that having investment decisions made by a full-time professional money manager will produce superior results compared to the returns that each member of the investment group has been able to accomplish individually.

Investors in the Grits Fund will be allocated ownership of the fund on the basis of their proportional contribution. Initially, there will be twenty owners, including yourself, who will each contribute a minimum of $10,000. The members have decided to issue the initial shares of ownership at a price of $10, although subsequent sales will occur at prices determined by the value of the company's portfolio of investments and the number of outstanding shares. The Grits Fund will accept investments from other individuals, and it will permit existing shareholders to purchase additional shares of stock. Likewise, shareholders may redeem, at any time, all or any portion of their shares. The method by which the fund's share price is established and the fund's shares are redeemed is addressed later in this chapter.

> **Tip** Remain alert to changes in a mutual fund's management. Management change may signal a new direction in portfolio management. Management change is especially troublesome when a fund has produced a long series of favorable returns.

Importance of the Fund's Investment Objective

It is crucial that your personal investment objectives are consistent with the objectives of the other members of your group and with the investment philosophy of the fund you will be joining. If most members of your group desire to have the fund invest in speculative stocks in the pursuit of high returns and you don't have the financial resources or the stomach for the potentially large losses that can result from this type of investing, you should look for a different investment. You should investigate a number of factors prior to investing in a mutual fund, but none is more important than the fund's investment objective.

Suppose that you and the other members of your investment group are unanimous in your desire to pursue a goal of capital growth with moderate risk. Current income is determined to be a secondary objective. The fund will achieve capital growth by investing in the stocks of companies that are market leaders and are expected to experience rising sales and earnings. The members decide to concentrate the fund's investments in the stocks of companies that operate primarily in the Southeast region of the United States because of the excellent business and political climate. Members inform the investment manager to keep brokerage commissions low by minimizing portfolio turnover.

Putting Together the Grits Fund

Suppose the 20 investors in your group contribute total investment capital of $400,000. Although you and some of the other investors have each decided to contribute only $10,000, several individuals will invest up to $40,000 each. The total combined investment will require that the fund initially issue 40,000 shares of stock valued at $10 each. The fund could equally well have issued 20,000 shares at a price of $20 each or 10,000 shares at a price of $40 each. You and the other investors choose an initial price of $10 because $10 seems to be a price that appeals to the majority of investors who purchase investment company shares.

Money contributed by the owners will be placed initially in highly liquid investments such as Treasury bills or a money market fund while the investment manager determines which stocks to acquire for the fund's portfolio. Balances in the short-term investments will gradually decline as money is withdrawn and invested in stocks chosen by the portfolio manager; however, the fund will need to maintain some short-term balances to pay its operating expenses (light bills, rent, telephone bills), to pay the investment manager's salary, and to pay for shares that are presented for redemption.

Tip Mutual funds occasionally go out of business by being merged into another mutual fund. A merger usually occurs when a mutual fund has exhibited poor investment performance and encountered difficulty attracting new investors. The fund eventually becomes too small to be profitable, at which point the sponsor may combine it with another fund.

The investment manager's view of the stock market is another factor that will influence the proportion of the fund's assets that is maintained in short-term investments.

A fund manager who believes the stock market is generally overvalued (i.e., that stock prices are too high) and poised for a decline is likely to maintain a substantial portion of the fund's assets in Treasury bills. When conditions have changed sufficiently to convince the manager that stocks have bottomed out and will be headed upward, the manager will sell the Treasury bills and use the proceeds to add growth stocks to the fund's portfolio. A fund manager who is optimistic about the stock market is likely to be fully invested in anticipation of increasing stock prices. A major part of a portfolio manager's job is determining the most favorable times to invest.

The Initial Portfolio

Suppose the investment manager decides to make the Grits Fund easier to manage (and easier for the author to explain) by limiting the fund's portfolio at any given time to no more than ten stocks. The limited portfolio of the Grits Fund compares to 50 to 100, or even more stocks that are owned by the typical mutual fund. Figure 5 (p. 32) displays the contents and value of the Grits Fund's initial portfolio.

Figure 5 indicates that of $400,000 initially contributed by investors, $370,449 has been invested in common stock and $27,649 remains in short-term investments such as Treasury bills or other money market securities. Brokerage commissions of approximately 0.5 percent of principal ($1,902) consumed the remainder of the initial shareholder contributions. For example, $39,250 that was invested in the stock of Bubba's Franks caused the fund to pay a brokerage commission of $196. The ten transactions resulted in the Grits Fund incurring bro-

Figure 5 ■ Initial Portfolio of the Grits Fund

Stock	Div.	Shares	Price	Value
Bubba's Franks	$ .56	1,000	$39.25	$39,250
Kudzu Exports	–	1,300	34.00	44,200
Boiled Peanuts, Inc.	.21	1,200	40.25	48,300
Greens R Us	.73	1,000	20.00	20,000
Fry It Or Else, Inc.	1.60	800	57.62	46,100
Catfish Ponds, Inc.	.12	600	59.00	35,400
Sister's Home Care	1.60	400	46.87	18,750
Dixie Dew Bottling	2.60	700	78.12	54,687
Ya'll Electric Co.	–	1,300	22.75	29,575
Graceland Reminders	1.32	500	68.32	34,187
Total Stock Portfolio Value				$370,449
Short-Term Investments				$27,649
Total Fund Value				$398,098
Shares Outstanding				40,000
Net Asset Value				$9.95

kerage commissions of $1,902, money that has been paid from the fund's initial $400,000 and is no longer available for investing.

Mutual fund shares are valued by calculating the net asset value (NAV), which is the total market value of the fund's assets (less any debts) divided by the number of the fund's outstanding shares. Figure 5 shows that the NAV of the Grits Fund is $398,098 divided by 40,000 shares, or $9.95. Net asset value establishes the price at which new shares will be offered to investors (unless a sales charge is added) and the price at which outstanding shares will be redeemed. A particular fund's NAV constantly changes as the securities held in the fund's portfolio fluctuate in price. An increase in the market prices of securities held in the fund's portfolio causes a corresponding increase in the net asset value of the fund's shares. Conversely, a decline in the prices of securities owned by the fund causes the fund's net asset value to fall.

In the unlikely event that the Grits Fund maintains exactly the same portfolio during the first year of operation, $6,014 in dividends will be received from the 10 securities that are owned (actually, only 8 of the 10 stocks pay dividends). Assuming all the dividends are passed through to the fund's stockholders, each of the fund's outstanding shares will earn a dividend of 15 cents ($6,014/40,000 shares). Thus, the 1,000 shares of the fund's stock that you purchased for an initial investment of $10,000 will earn $150 of dividends during the first year you hold the stock. The current return on your initial investment is $150 in annual dividends divided by $10,000, or 1.5 percent. This is a modest current return, but you must take into consideration the fact that the fund's goal is growth in value, not current income.

Tip The net asset value of a mutual fund is only as accurate as the accuracy of the valuations for securities held by the fund. Some securities seldom trade and have limited liquidity, making them difficult to value or, alternatively, easy to overvalue.

How Changes in Stock Prices Affect Net Asset Value

Suppose twelve months pass and the composition of the Grits Fund portfolio remains unchanged. Although the fund continues to hold the same securities, the market value of each of the stocks has changed. The new stock prices and portfolio value are illustrated in Figure 6.

The $19,325 increase in the market value of the fund's securities results in $417,423 of total fund assets and a net asset value of $417,423/40,000 shares, or $10.44. You now own 1,000 shares worth $10.44 each, for a total value of $10,440. You have earned a total profit of $150 (15 cents per share in dividends paid to you by the fund) plus $440 in the appreciation of your shares ($10,440 current value less your $10,000 original investment), or $590. This represents a 5.9 percent return on your original $10,000 investment.

The fund's investment income and dividends to shareholders will actually be lower than what is indicated here because there has been no accounting for expenses to operate and manage the fund. For example, the cost of employing the investment manager, paying the telephone bills, and so forth would ordinarily have to be paid from the fund's investment income, thereby reducing the dividends paid to the Grits Fund's shareholders. If the fund incurred expenses of $5,000, total dividends paid to shareholders would have been $1,014 rather than $6,014.

The Effect of Portfolio Changes on Net Asset Value

Portfolio turnover has no effect on net asset value except insomuch as (1) brokerage commissions paid by the fund to buy and sell securities reduce NAV, and (2) different securities can be expected to experience different price changes, thus influencing future changes in the fund's NAV. If an investment manager replaces several securities with other securities that subse-

Figure 6 ■ Valuation of the Grits Fund After One Year

Stock	Div.	Shares	Price	Value
Bubba's Franks	$ .56	1,000	$45.50	$ 45,500
Kudzu Exports	-	1,300	36.12	46,962
Boiled Peanuts, Inc.	.21	1,200	40.50	48,600
Greens R Us	.73	1,000	25.12	25,125
Fry It Or Else, Inc.	1.60	800	56.50	45,200
Catfish Ponds, Inc.	.12	600	62.38	37,425
Sister's Home Care	1.60	400	46.00	18,400
Dixie Dew Bottling	2.60	700	84.50	59,150
Ya'll Electric Co.	-	1,300	20.75	26,975
Graceland Reminders	1.32	500	70.88	35,437
Total Stock Portfolio Value				$388,774
Short-Term Investments				28,649
Total Fund Value				$417,423
Shares Outstanding				40,000
Net Asset Value				$10.44

quently increase proportionately more in price than the securities that were sold, the fund's NAV and your investment in the fund will benefit with higher values.

To observe how swapping securities leaves the fund's net asset value unaffected, suppose at the end of the year the investment manager sells all the Bubba's Franks stock and the Ya'll Electric stock held by the fund. The manager will probably transfer the $72,475 proceeds received from the sale into short-term securities and subsequently reinvest in other stocks. Other than brokerage commissions that the fund must pay, neither the sale of the two stock positions nor the reinvestment of the proceeds in different assets has any immediate effect on the total assets in the fund's portfolio and no effect on the fund's net asset value. Switching from one stock to another, or from a stock to a short-term investment, reallocates the portfolio's assets, but it does not increase or reduce the total value of the portfolio.

The Effect on NAV of Selling and Redeeming Shares of the Fund's Stock

Your investment in a mutual fund remains unaffected when the fund issues additional shares of stock or redeems a portion of the fund's outstanding shares so long as the net asset value is used to price the shares that are sold or redeemed. Because changes in outstanding shares will not affect your financial position, you generally have no cause for concern when new investors purchase shares of the fund or when current stockholders exit the fund by cashing in their shares.

Selling Additional Shares of the Fund's Stock

As mentioned previously, the managers of a mutual fund receive compensation based on the amount of assets they supervise. Their compensation is generally established as a percentage of the assets in the fund's portfolio, although the percentage fee may be scheduled to decline somewhat as the total assets surpass specified levels. The assets in a portfolio increase as individual securities held by the fund increase in price and as investors purchase additional shares of the fund. Thus, it is to the investment managers' financial advantage to produce above-average investment performance that increases the market value of assets being managed at the same time it attracts new investors to the fund.

Issuing new shares of the Grits Fund to existing or outside investors will not change the value of your own shares because it will not change the fund's net asset value. Suppose we consider an instance in which a new investor purchases 1,000 shares of the fund's stock. The fund issues 1,000 additional shares, causing the fund's total outstanding shares to increase from 40,000 to 41,000. The new investor is required to pay $10,440, or $10.44 per share, the current net asset value, for each share purchased. Following the issue of the new shares, the fund owns a portfolio valued at $417,423 plus the new investor's contribution of $10,440, or $427,863. The net asset value remains at $427,863 divided by 11,000 shares, or $10.44.

The investment manager must find a use for the new money invested in the fund, which means that more shares of stock must be added to the fund's portfolio. The new money may be placed temporarily in short-term investments while various stock investments are evaluated, or the money may be invested immediately in shares of stock. The manager will not normally want a large portion of the fund's portfolio in short-term assets that earn relatively low returns, especially given the fund's investment objective of capital growth.

Redeeming the Fund's Outstanding Shares

Share redemptions have the opposite effect on the fund's portfolio compared to sales of additional shares. Redemptions require that the investment manager pay money to the selling stockholders in return for retiring the shares presented for redemption. If a relatively small number of shares are redeemed, short-term investments are tapped to provide the necessary money. Otherwise, the investment manager must sell shares from the fund's stock portfolio to raise the required amount of money.

Suppose a stockholder decides to sell 2,000 shares back to the Grits Fund at the end of the first year of operation. The mutual fund's investment manager must come up with $20,880 (2,000 shares at a NAV of $10.44), an amount that is somewhat less than the $28,649 the fund has available in short-term investments. The investment manager could redeem the 2,000 shares without selling any stock from the fund's portfolio. On the other hand, the manager may feel that the fund should always maintain adequate liquidity that requires holding at least $20,000 in short-term assets.

To meet the self-established liquidity requirement, the investment manager decides to sell the fund's entire 400-share position in Sister's Home Care common stock, which nets $18,400 for the fund. When $18,400 in proceeds from the stock sale are added to existing short-term assets of $28,649, total short-term investments climb to $47,049. To this point there is no change in the net asset value of the Grits Fund because total fund assets and shares outstanding each remain unchanged. The fund manager has merely transferred $18,400 from common stock to short-term investments.

While portfolio turnover does not affect either fund assets or outstanding shares of the fund, selling or redeeming shares of the fund changes both these variables. When the fund pays out $20,880 for 2,000 shares of its own stock, total fund assets will decline by $20,880, to $396,543, while outstanding shares of the fund's stock will drop by 2,000 to 38,000. Even though the fund's total assets and shares outstanding are each reduced as a result of the redemption, the net asset value of the fund remains at $10.44 because the reduction in assets is exactly offset by a proportional reduction in outstanding shares. Neither the sale of additional shares nor the redemption of outstanding shares

Figure 7 ■ **Effect of Shareholder Redemption**

	Year-End Values	After Stock Sale	After Redemption
Short-Term Investments	$ 28,649	$ 47,049	$ 26,169
Stock Portfolio	$ 388,774	$ 370,374	$ 370,374
Total Fund Assets	$ 417,423	$ 417,423	$ 396,543
Shares Outstanding	40,000	40,000	38,000
Net Asset Value	$10.44	$10.44	$10.44

affects the net asset value of a mutual fund's shares. A summary of the effects of the transactions just discussed is illustrated in Figure 7.

Thus, portfolio turnover, share redemptions, and the sale of additional shares do not have a discernible effect on the Grits Fund's net asset value, the measure of the fund's value that is most important to you and the other shareholders. New investors can buy into the fund and current investors can liquidate their shares without disturbing your own investment in the fund. Portfolio turnover will have some effect because the fund pays brokerage commissions when stocks are bought and sold. Also, redemptions and sales of new shares sometimes have an effect on the way a fund is managed. As funds grow larger, their portfolio managers lose flexibility in the investments they can choose.

The Effect of Dividends and Capital Gains Distributions

Sales and redemptions of the fund's shares do not affect your investment in the mutual fund because they do not affect the value of a fund's assets on a per-share basis. On the other hand, distributions by a mutual fund do affect your investment. Both

> ### Tip
> Distribution of dividends and capital gains will cause a decrease in a mutual fund's net asset value because following a distribution the fund will have fewer assets but the same number of outstanding shares. A distribution is really nothing other than a transfer of assets from the fund to the shareholders who are likely to be required to pay taxes on the distribution.

dividend payments and capital gain distributions reduce a mutual fund's net asset value.

Dividend Payments

A dividend payment to a company's stockholders reduces the price of the firm's stock by the amount of the dividend payment. For example, a 75-cent dividend to stockholders causes the price of the firm's common stock to fall by an equal amount, three-quarters of a point. The stock price declines because the dividend payment leaves the company with a smaller amount of assets on which to earn income in subsequent periods. Your overall wealth as a stockholder of the firm is unaffected by a dividend payment because the reduction in the value of your stock is offset by the dividend that is received.

If the wealth of individual stockholders is not affected by dividend payments, the wealth of a mutual fund, which is itself a stockholder, is also unaffected by dividend payments on the stocks that it holds in its portfolio, at least initially. When a stock owned by a mutual fund pays a dividend, the mutual fund's stock portfolio declines in value (because the stock on which the dividend is paid declines in market price) at the same time that the fund's short-term investments are supplemented by the dividend received. Thus, the fund's net asset value and your investment in the fund are unaffected by dividend payments to the mutual fund.

So how is your investment in a mutual fund affected when the mutual fund pays a dividend to you and its other stockholders? It was mentioned earlier that mutual funds typically pass through to their own stockholders all, or nearly all, the dividends and interest they receive. The effect of a mutual fund's dividend payment is identical to the effect of a dividend payment on an individual stock that you own. That is, the value of your investment in the fund will decline by the amount of the dividend you receive. Suppose you own 200 shares in a mutual fund that has a net asset value of $14.50 per share. If the fund pays a dividend of 75 cents per share, the fund's net asset value will decline by 75 cents, to $13.75 per share. The total value of your shares declines by $150 (75 cents times 200 shares), a sum that is identical to the dividend income you receive. Thus, your total wealth is unchanged since you now have more cash (the dividend) that is offset by a lower net asset value of the mutual fund shares.

Capital Gains Distributions

Realized gains from securities sold by a mutual fund do not affect the value of the fund's net asset value until the gains are distributed to shareholders. The distribution of gains has the same effect as the payment of dividends. That is, a capital gain

Tip Mutual funds that hold a portfolio of mostly foreign securities have a net asset value that is affected not only by the market value of the foreign securities, but also by currency exchange rates. Owning a mutual fund that holds securities valued in a foreign currency creates the potential for added gains or losses depending upon what happens to currency exchange rates during the period you hold shares in the fund.

distribution reduces the assets of the fund and the net asset value of the fund's shares. The NAV reduction is equal to the amount of the realized gain that is distributed to shareholders. If a mutual fund pays a $1.20 per share capital gain distribution, the fund's total assets will decline by $1.20 times the number of outstanding shares, and the net asset value will decline by $1.20 per share. The cash distribution by the fund reduces the value of your investment in the fund by the amount of the distribution you receive. Thus, you are no better off or worse off after the capital gains distribution than you were before the distribution. Well, sort of.

Taxation of Distributions

The problem with dividends and capital gains distributions is that you will be taxed on the money you receive (unless you receive dividends from a fund that invests in tax-exempt securities). Thus, a distribution causes you to incur a tax liability that reduces the value of your total wealth because the amount of additional cash you have left after taxes will be less than the declines in the value of your mutual fund shares. Suppose you buy shares of a mutual fund just prior to a major capital gains distribution. You receive the distribution causing the net asset value of your shares to decline by an offsetting amount. However, you now have a tax liability on the distribution you received that will cause a reduction in your overall wealth.

You would be in a better financial position if the mutual fund reinvested the dividends it received rather than passing them along to you. However, special tax exemptions are accorded only to mutual funds that distribute the dividends they receive to their shareholders. Somebody has to pay for the gains that are realized and with mutual fund investments it is you, not the fund that pays.

3 Equity Funds

E quity funds—mutual funds that invest in common stocks—have been, until recent years, the clear choice of individual investors who trusted their money to the care of investment companies. Although equity funds (also called *stock funds* and *common stock funds*) are often subject to substantial fluctuations in value, investors are attracted to the large potential returns that can be earned from common stock ownership. Different categories of stock funds provide different investment returns and subject mutual fund shareholders to different risks. It is important to select an equity fund that has an investment goal that is compatible with your own financial needs.

When you read an article or overhear a discussion about mutual funds, your thoughts are likely to turn to common stocks even though mutual funds that specialize in equity ownership comprise only a little over a third of all investment companies. The connection between mutual funds and common stocks is to some extent caused by the large price changes of equity fund shares and the resulting fanfare these funds receive in the media. Just as bettors at a horse track talk mostly about the long shots they hit, mutual fund investors are more prone to discuss the 10 to 20 percent returns they earn from common stock funds than the 5 percent returns from bond funds or the

2 percent earned from money market funds. Although individuals are less likely to talk about major losses of any kind, the financial media have never been shy about reporting on equity funds that sustain large losses in value. In short, stock funds are where the action is! Figure 8 illustrates the increase in the assets managed by equity funds. Notice that equity assets peaked in 1999 and 2000 before being depleted by a declining stock market and disgruntled investors.

Historically, equity funds have been the investment of choice among investors. It was not until the mid 1980s that equity funds were surpassed by bond and income funds in both the number of funds and the amount of assets under management. Many investors who choose to invest by way of mutual funds are interested in equity funds because of the potentially large returns they can earn from owning common stocks. Also, common stocks are relatively difficult securities to value, and many individual investors prefer to turn over to professional money managers the decisions regarding which stocks to buy and what prices to pay. What better way to obtain professional guidance than to buy into a stock portfolio managed by an experienced portfolio manager?

Fundamentals of Common Stocks

Shares of common stock represent units of ownership in a corporation. The more shares issued by a particular corporation, the smaller the proportional ownership a single share represents. If you own 100 shares of the stock of a company that has 10 million outstanding shares, you own 100/10,000,000, or .001 percent of the company. If you hold 100 shares of the stock of a company that has 1,000 outstanding shares, you own 10 percent of the company. The greater the percentage that you

Figure 8 ■ Assets Managed by Equity Funds, 1975–2002

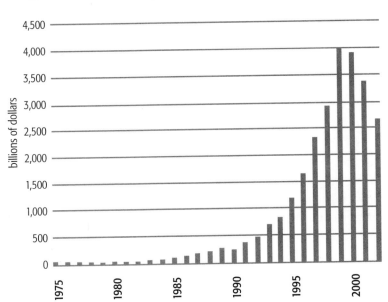

own of a company's stock, the more influence you are likely to have on the company's operations.

A company issues shares of common stock in order to raise capital to acquire buildings, purchase equipment, pay employees, buy materials, and so forth. In return for providing capital, common stockholders acquire an ownership interest in the company's assets and, more importantly, a claim to whatever income remains after all other obligations have been satisfied. Employees, suppliers, lenders, and state and local tax authorities all must be paid before a firm's stockholders have a claim to anything. Common stockholders are said to have a residual claim because all other claims come first. On the positive side, a successful company can pay all its other claims and still have a great deal of money left for the owners.

The Value of Common Stock

Owners of common stock stand to benefit when a company's managers invest in assets that earn the firm substantial profits. If a company is able to utilize its assets to develop a widely needed drug, a highly efficient engine, a very comfortable and long-wearing shoe, or a more tasty ice cream, the company and its owners stand to gain great financial rewards. On the other hand, stockholders are likely to suffer financial losses when a firm's managers make poor use of the company's financial and physical resources. A series of investment blunders by a firm's managers may leave stockholders with nothing to share after all the company's other claimants have been paid. The stockholders of a company can earn a return on their own investment in two ways: (1) from dividends that are periodically distributed to shareholders from the firm's profits, and (2) from increases in the market price of shares of the firm's stock. A company's directors are charged with determining the firm's dividend distributions to owners. The decision is generally made quarterly and must take into account the firm's need for expansion capital in relation to current profits. Companies that have only modest needs for additional assets often pay a large portion of their earnings in dividends. The directors of a rapidly growing company that requires large amounts of capital to pay for additional assets may decide to forego any dividend distribution to stockholders and retain all of the firm's profits for reinvestment. Companies that reinvest most or all of their earnings in additional assets cause their stockholders to sacrifice current dividend income in return for the likelihood of increased future profits. The directors and stockholders hope that increased profits will translate into a higher price for the firm's stock.

The second potential source of stockholder income is an increase in the value of the shares of stock they own. The term

> **Tip** Don't select a mutual fund based on its most recent short-term performance. Returns during the last three months or one year tend to be a poor predictor of how a fund will perform in the future. Long-term performance is a superior measure of how a mutual fund stacks up against the competition.

potential is appropriate because a stock's price may increase, but then again it may decline or not change in value at all. A firm's stock price can decline enough to more than offset dividend income, thereby causing stockholders of a firm to suffer an overall loss. In most years changes in the value of stock, either positive or negative, will overwhelm any dividend income.

Many factors influence a company's stock price, but none is more important than the investment community's expectations regarding the firm's future profits. An improved profit outlook will usually increase a firm's common stock price. Conversely, investors surprised by a company's announcement of a problem such as management turnover, plant closures, or falling sales are likely to revise their earnings forecasts downward and cause the firm's stock price to decline. Stock prices are also strongly influenced by interest rate changes. Rising interest rates tend to push stock prices downward while falling interest rates cause stock prices to rise.

Not all stock prices move together, even during major movements in the overall stock market. For example, the common stocks of some large, established companies are valued for stable earnings and dividends that cause the stocks' prices to be relatively stable compared to the overall stock market. Some stocks (e.g., utilities) are strongly affected by interest rate movements while other stocks (e.g., defense firms, construction firms) are impacted more by government policy. Because stocks do not always move in tandem, the return earned from common stocks is often as much a function of the particular stocks that are owned as of general stock market movements.

The Risks of Owning Common Stock

Common stock investments (and mutual funds that invest in common stocks) can produce impressive returns, but you also assume substantial risks by owning these financial assets. Common stocks are very difficult to value precisely because so many variables influence common stock prices. For example, your favorable impression of a company's product line may cause you to consider an investment in the firm's common stock. Further investigation of the company's financial statement indicates minimal debt and an impressive string of earnings increases. Everything seems to be in order. Unfortunately, you may not realize that a much larger firm is preparing to introduce a competing product line of equal or better quality that will sell at a lower price. Suddenly, a company with excellent prospects may turn into a business that has to fight for its survival. Just ask the supermarket chains that have had to compete with Wal-Mart. A decade ago, the firm was not a player in this market. Now it is a ferocious competitor. Numerous firms that pioneered the personal computer market are now out of business. Owning shares of common stock is inherently risky because so many factors influence the value of a company and its stock.

Stock prices tend to be very volatile, and the prices of some stocks may bounce up or down by as much as 5 to 10 percent in a single day's trading. The stock prices of airline companies, automotive companies, and companies in many other cyclical industries are subject to major price swings that can cause large gains and losses for stockholders. Telecom companies could do no wrong in the late 1990s and their stocks rose to the heavens.

> **Tip** Don't assume that a mutual fund, especially an equity fund, is a low-risk investment. Equity funds provide varying degrees of diversification and can experience dramatic changes in market value.

A few years later they could do no right and their stocks sank out of sight. Substantial price volatility is an important risk, especially if you may be required to liquidate an investment on short notice.

Stock price volatility stems in part from the fact that expectations regarding a company's future profits—the major variable influencing a company's stock price—are subject to constant and sudden revisions. Even relatively small changes in a company's revenues can cause major changes in the firm's profits. Unexpected changes in current earnings, in turn, can alarm investors who anticipated better results. Investors surprised by a decline in a company's reported earnings are likely to start selling the stock, driving the price down. Investors can be expected to buy the firm's common stock and drive its price up when earnings are higher than expected.

In the event a company runs into serious competitive, operational, or financial difficulties, causing its sales and profits to shrink, the firm's management may find it necessary to reduce or eliminate the dividend, an action that may precipitate a major decline in the common stock price. A company can lose money for only so long before it becomes unable even to pay its creditors. If a company encounters an unfavorable business environment for an extended period of time, its accumulated losses may be so great that the stockholders' investment is completely wiped out. The liquidation of a financially ailing company is one of the worst possible outcomes for the firm's stockholders, of course, but it can and does occur, especially in a weak economy. Even major companies including United Airlines, WorldCom, and Kmart were forced to file for bankruptcy.

Influences on Equity Fund Values

Chapter 2 discussed factors that influence the net asset value of a mutual fund's shares. At any particular time, an equity fund's overall value equals the cumulative value of the stocks owned (stock price times number of shares) plus the cash equivalents that are in the fund's portfolio awaiting investment. The net asset value of an equity fund is the current value of all of the fund's assets (less any debts) divided by the fund's outstanding shares. Issuing additional shares or redeeming outstanding shares of an equity fund causes no change in the fund's net asset value because the increase or decrease in the fund's assets is exactly offset by a proportional increase or decrease in the number of outstanding shares.

Changes in Net Asset Value

Changes in the prices of stocks held in a mutual fund's portfolio will affect both the value of the fund's portfolio and, more importantly, the net asset value of the fund's shares. You can expect major upward movement in the stock market to be accompanied by an increase in the prices of most stocks held in a mutual fund's portfolio. An increase in the value of a fund's assets caused by rising stock prices is independent of the outstanding shares and will cause an increase in the fund's net asset value. Likewise, a general downward movement in the stock market tends to cause a decline in the net asset value of an equity fund because the prices of stocks owned by the fund are likely to decline. In short, equity fund share prices (the net asset values) are driven by the prices of the common stocks these funds own.

Changes in an equity fund's net asset value depend both upon the particular stocks a fund owns and on movements in the stock market. If an equity fund owns the "right" stocks, the fund's net asset value will increase proportionately more than the overall stock market when the market is rising and will decrease proportionately less than the overall stock market when the market is falling. (The Standard & Poor's 500 Index is often used as a proxy for the overall stock market.) Unfortunately, the "right" stocks are very difficult to identify, even for professional portfolio managers.

Portfolio Management and Changes in Net Asset Value

Ideally, an equity fund manager will invest all the fund's assets in stocks that react strongly to overall market movements just prior to a major upward move in the market. Prior to a major dip in the market, the manager would alter the composition of the fund's portfolio by lightening up on stocks (i.e., decreasing the proportion of the fund's assets invested in stocks) and by moving into more conservative stocks. To accomplish this, a portfolio manager must be able to accurately forecast stock market movements, a task that many market researchers believe is, at best, very difficult.

In general, equity funds that hold specialized portfolios are subject to larger proportional gains and losses in net asset values compared to equity funds that hold diversified portfolios. For example, equity funds that specialize in the common stocks of companies that operate in a particular industry or a particular country subject their shareholders to much greater risks than equity funds that hold a large variety of stocks because stocks of similar companies tend to move together. Unexpected events can strike an individual industry as well as an individual company. Witness the disastrous consequences to the airline industry from the September 11, 2001, terrorist attacks on the United States.

Substantial research indicates that even professional portfolio managers, individuals who are paid hefty salaries to know such things, have difficulty forecasting stock price movements with any degree of accuracy. Aggressive equity funds that outperform a rising stock market tend to underperform (show greater proportional losses) a falling stock market. Conservative equity funds that tend to outperform a declining stock market (show smaller proportional losses) generally underperform the market during periods of rising stock prices. Most researchers who study the returns earned by mutual funds believe that the relative performance of an equity fund (i.e., the returns earned by a fund's shareholders compared to those returns earned by shareholders of other funds) in one year is of little or no value in forecasting the relative performance of the fund in the following year.

Types of Equity Funds

Equity funds are classified according to the investment objectives the funds pursue. The objectives, in turn, determine the types of securities that equity funds buy and hold in their portfolios. Mutual funds that seek to maximize capital growth invest in stocks that offer the potential for achieving large price gains. Ownership of these stocks nearly always entails substantial risks. The stocks of companies that can provide explosive growth nearly always carry some unwanted baggage: untried technology, recent rapid run-ups in the stock prices, high price-earnings ratios, uncertain markets, or the possibility of cutthroat competition. Other funds concentrate more on providing their stock-holders with current income. These funds offer greater price stability but with a reduced likelihood that large gains in value will occur.

You should strive to select a fund with an investment objective that is compatible with your own investment goals. Just as a young single person or a middle-aged couple is unlikely to want to invest all of their money in a fund that provides mostly current dividend income, a retired couple is unlikely to want a large portion of their money invested in an aggressive growth fund because substantial losses could result.

Some financial advisers suggest that your money be spread among a number of different funds with different investment goals. For example, you might want to invest in both an equity-income fund and a growth fund. Always remember that it is wise to hedge your bets. No matter how strongly you believe stocks are headed for a major rise in value, you may be wrong. Just as the three most important determinants of real estate value are location, location, and location, the three most important words of advice in stock market investing are diversify, diversify, and diversify. Figure 9 (p.54) identifies the investment objectives of the country's ten largest equity funds as of the end of 2002.

Tip Substantial differences exist in operating expenses among equity funds. Growth funds operated by portfolio managers who frequently trade securities are likely to have operating expenses of three to four times the operating expenses of an index fund. Operating expenses are a direct reduction in the return earned by shareholders.

Figure 9 ■ **Ten Largest Equity Funds, Dec. 31, 2002**

Fund	Assets (millions)	Investment Objective
Fidelity Magellan Fund	$56,751	Growth
Vanguard 500 Index	56,224	Growth/Income
Investment Company of America	46,129	Growth/Income
Washington Mutual Investors	42,436	Growth/Income
Growth Fund of America	31,105	Growth
Fidelity Contrafund	27,695	Growth
Fidelity Growth & Income	26,269	Growth/Income
Europacific Growth Fund	22,601	Foreign Equity
New Perspective Fund	22,166	Global Equity
Income Fund of America	20,979	Income

Although one or more mutual funds are available for virtually any investment taste, no matter how specialized, the thousands of equity funds fall into one of several classifications. These are:

Capital appreciation funds Capital appreciation funds concentrate on investing in the common stocks of small or well-established companies with the potential to produce substantial capital gains for stockholders. In general, these funds concentrate on capital appreciation, not current dividend income. One segment of this category, *aggressive growth funds*, specializes in owning the stocks of small growth companies. These funds experience large price volatility and provide little, if any, dividend income to their shareholders. *Growth funds* invest primarily in the stocks of well-established companies that offer the potential for substantial growth in earnings. Although growth funds invest in the stocks of companies that portfolio managers believe will produce long-term price appreciation, these funds tend to avoid the high-risk stocks favored by aggressive growth funds. Growth funds experience less price volatility than aggressive growth funds. The third type of capital appreciation fund, *sector funds*, invests primarily in the stocks of companies in related fields. For example, a fund might concentrate on owning stocks of companies engaged in telecommunications or companies involved in precious metals. Unlike equity funds that reduce risk by diversifying their portfolios across a large number of industries, sector funds attract investors who seek to limit their investment to a particular industry. These funds can exhibit unusual volatility because of the lack of diversification.

Total return funds Funds in this category seek a compromise between current income and capital appreciation. *Growth and income funds* invest in common stocks that offer good possibilities for growing revenues and profits but also pay relatively high dividends. These funds tend to buy the stocks of mature companies that still have the potential for growing revenues and earnings. Growth and income funds hold relatively conservative portfolios that provide less growth than growth funds and less income than funds that concentrate on high-dividend stocks. *Income-equity funds* attempt to provide shareholders with a high

> **Tip** Sector funds provide limited diversification because they hold specialized portfolios. The lack of diversification subjects sector fund shareholders to substantial risk compared to more broad-based funds that invest in a wide variety of industries and geographic regions.

level of current income by investing in common stocks that pay dividends that are relatively large compared to the respective stock prices. Common stocks with high dividend returns generally have a limited potential for capital gains. Thus, income-equity funds are an appropriate choice if you are more interested in current income than in capital growth. Movements in long-term interest rates have a major influence on the net asset values of income-equity funds.

World equity funds World equity funds invest primarily in the stocks of foreign companies and allow investors to own the common stocks of foreign companies without the hassle of exchanging currencies or paying unusually high commissions. These funds provide excellent diversification because at any given time security prices often move differently in different countries. For example, stock markets in Europe and Asia may be strong at the same time that stocks in the United States are weak. Likewise, overseas markets may be weak when U.S. stocks are strong. Shares traded in foreign securities markets are denominated in foreign currencies, causing the returns of funds that invest in these securities to be influenced both by changes in the market values of the stocks (as denominated in each stock's respective currency) and by the rate at which the foreign currencies can be exchanged for dollars. Mutual funds with large holdings of foreign securities are negatively affected by a strengthening U.S. dollar and positively affected by a weakening U.S. dollar. World equity funds include *emerging market funds* that invest primarily in developing regions of the world. These funds can have very volatile net asset values but offer the potential for very large gains. Keep in mind that stocks in emerging countries often have limited liquidity and companies may be subject to minimal financial reporting requirements. *Regional equity funds* specialize in the stocks of companies based in a specific region of the world. For example, a fund may restrict its portfolio holdings to the stocks of companies in Western Europe or the Pacific Rim. *Global equity funds* invest in the common stocks of foreign companies as well as the common stocks of U.S. companies. Global funds allow investors to participate in the ownership of foreign companies that may have superior growth prospects compared to many domestic companies. *International funds* invest in the common stocks of companies located outside the United States. Like global funds, international funds provide returns based on a combination of (1) the returns provided by the portfolio's stocks in the countries in which they are traded, and (2) the rate at which the foreign currencies exchange for the dollar.

Hybrid funds Hybrid funds invest in a combination of fixed-income securities, equities, and derivatives. In general, these funds seek higher levels of current income than capital appreciation funds or world equity funds. *Balanced funds* hold portfolios comprised of common stocks, preferred stocks, and bonds. Balanced funds seek a compromise between current income and growth by investing in a combination of securities that provides some income and the possibility for some growth. Common stocks provide the potential of an increase in net asset value at the same time that interest from bonds and dividends from preferred stocks allow a balanced fund to pay a moderate dividend to its shareholders. Balanced funds generally under-perform a strong stock market and out-perform a weak stock market. Shares in balanced funds are suitable for relatively conservative investors. *Asset allocation funds* invest in predetermined asset classes according to established weightings. For example, an asset allocation fund may choose to have 40 percent of assets in equities, 40 percent in bonds, and 20 percent in money market instruments. *Flexible portfolio funds* invest in a combination of

> **Tip** Equity funds that attempt to track a particular stock index tend to have low portfolio turnover, low expenses, and minimal tax consequences for shareholders. Low portfolio turnover means less management time and fewer security sales that would produce capital gains distributions.

common stocks, debt securities, and money market securities in an attempt to provide high total return. These funds have the flexibility to concentrate all of their assets in a single type of security. *Income-mixed funds* invest in income-producing securities in seeking to provide a high level of current income.

Index funds Although not always considered a separate class of mutual funds, index funds have become so popular that they deserve a discussion. Index funds assemble portfolios in an attempt to match the returns of the overall stock market or a segment of the stock market as measured by a particular index. For example, a mutual fund may attempt to duplicate the returns of the Standard & Poor's 500 or the Russell 2000. The philosophy of an index fund is that mutual fund managers have historically had a difficult time consistently out-performing the market, so why try? An index fund minimizes the expenses of research and trading by assembling and maintaining a portfolio that emulates the overall market or a particular segment of the market. Index funds require little portfolio management and generally reward investors with low expenses. Many financial planners believe that for most investors index funds are the best choice among all types of mutual funds.

4   Bond Funds

Bond funds invest their owners' money in the debt securities of businesses and governmental organizations. Bond funds are of primary interest to conservative investors who seek relatively high current income. The values of bond funds, especially funds that own bonds with long maturities, are primarily driven by market interest rates. The net asset values of bond funds move inversely with interest rates. In general, bond funds are subject to smaller variations in market value than are equity funds.

Mutual funds that specialize in bond investments came of age in the mid 1980s as investors chased the high current returns offered by corporate and government bonds. Figure 10 (p. 60) illustrates that net assets in bond funds exploded from $46 billion in 1984 to $1,184 billion less than two decades later. Although bonds are generally easier to value than common stocks, a diversified portfolio of individual bond issues requires a substantial monetary investment, so many individuals find it

> **Tip**
>
> Bond funds tend to exhibit more stability and produce greater current returns than equity funds. On the other hand, bond funds offer less potential for gains in net asset value.

Figure 10 ■ Assets Managed by Bond Funds, 1984–2002

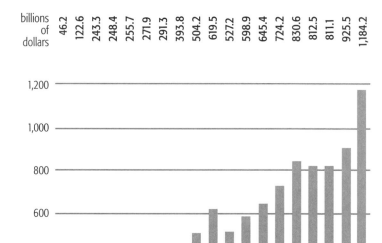

more convenient and affordable to invest in the shares of bond funds than to purchase individual bond issues.

Bond funds are ongoing companies that continually reinvest the proceeds from securities that are sold or redeemed. Continuous reinvestment of the proceeds from security sales means there is not a specified date on which shareholders in a bond fund are scheduled to have their money returned as would occur if individual bond issues were owned. Bonds mature, but bond funds do not. Only the bonds owned by bond funds mature, and the money received from matured bonds is reinvested in other bonds.

> **Tip** Investing in a bond fund as opposed to buying individual bonds means you are unable to target a date on which your principal will be returned. Bond funds continually reinvest proceeds from redeemed bonds, meaning that you will have to sell shares in the fund in order to have your principal returned. Unfortunately, there is no way to know exactly how much principal will be returned.

Bond funds pay higher current returns and vary less in value than most equity funds. The higher current return paid by bond funds results from the higher current yields from bond interest payments compared to the dividend yields on common stocks. The relative stability of bond fund net asset values results from the general price stability of bonds. A mutual fund that owns securities that exhibit stable market prices will have a stable net asset value. The investment goals and investment performance of bond funds attract mostly conservative investors who seek relatively large amounts of current income. The potential for capital gains is more limited than with mutual funds that invest in common stocks.

Fundamentals of Bonds

A bond is evidence of debt on the part of the security's issuer. Investors who purchase bonds become creditors of the organization that issued the bonds. Bonds have a stated maturity date on which the principal amount owed on the debt is scheduled for full repayment. Between the time bonds are issued and the time they are redeemed, the issuer is generally required to make a series of fixed semiannual interest payments, in amounts determined by the stated interest rate (called the *coupon* or *coupon rate*) and the principal amount of the debt (called the *par* or *par value*). For example, a 7-percent coupon, $1,000-par bond requires that the issuer pay $70 in annual interest (7 percent of $l,000) for each outstanding bond. Payments are in semiannual installments of $35 for as long as the bond remains outstanding. A 9-percent coupon, $1,000 principal amount bond will pay annual interest of $90 in the form of two $45 semiannual payments.

Corporate bonds are nearly always denominated in $1,000 amounts while bonds issued by cities and states (termed *municipal bonds* or *munis*) are generally denominated in $5,000 amounts. The owner of a $5,000 principal amount, 5-percent coupon municipal bond will receive $250 of annual interest. U.S. government securities are issued in various denominations depending upon the particular type of bond. Treasury bills (U.S. Treasury securities with original maturities of one year or less) are denominated in $10,000 amounts while long-term Treasury bonds are denominated in $1,000 amounts. Federal agency securities are issued in $5,000 denominations.

Organizations borrow money for many reasons. Corporations issue bonds in order to obtain money to acquire additional assets or to pay off outstanding debt. Bond issues are an alternative to issuing preferred stock or diluting ownership by issuing additional shares of common stock. Governments issue bonds when tax revenues are insufficient to cover spending. The federal government sometimes finds it necessary to annually borrow hundreds of billions of dollars to pay for spending that is in excess of its tax revenues. Likewise, cities and states issue bonds to pay for parks, bridges, water systems, rapid transit systems, stadiums, and a variety of other needs. The federal government and state and local governments also issue bonds in order to raise the money to pay off outstanding bonds that reach maturity.

Bonds create a legal obligation on the part of the borrower to make the specified interest payments and to repay the debt's principal amount at maturity. Interest and principal payments on corporate debt have priority over payments of any kind to a firm's stockholders. Payments to creditors must be made in full and on time, or legal action is likely to be initiated by the creditors. In contrast, payments to a company's shareholders are at the discretion of a firm's directors. The priority of debt obligations allows bondholders more confidence than stockholders regarding how much money they will receive and when the money will be paid.

How Bonds Are Valued

A bond is valued for the cash payments of interest and principal that are promised to the bondholders. A bond is more valuable the higher its promised interest payments, the larger the amount of the principal repayment, and the greater the certainty that these payments will be made in full and on schedule. The length of time before a bond is scheduled for redemption can significantly influence a bond's value. The degree to which maturity length influences a bond's price depends upon how the bond's coupon rate compares to the current market rate of interest on bonds of similar risk and maturity.

Both the creditworthiness of the issuer and the specific assets (if any) that are pledged as collateral affect a bond's credit quality. A bond with the weak guarantee of a company that is encountering substantial financial difficulties is likely to have a price that is heavily penalized by investors unless the bond carries a relatively high coupon rate. Investors who prefer high-quality bonds that are certain to be repaid must be willing to accept a reduced amount of annual interest income.

Bond investors generally rely on credit ratings supplied by

three major rating agencies that are in the business of judging a borrower's creditworthiness. These agencies consider management quality, profitability, revenue forecasts, existing interest obligations, and many other factors when they develop a bond issue's quality rating. Ratings supplied by the rating agencies play a major role in determining the interest rate a borrower must pay in order to issue bonds to investors. The credit ratings and their respective meanings are shown in Figure 11.

Bond values are primarily affected by changes in market rates of interest. Rising interest rates cause a decline in the prices of outstanding bonds, and falling interest rates cause these same bonds to increase in price. Suppose in 1993 you purchased a $10,000 principal amount bond with a 2017 maturity. You have received $1,000 (10 percent of $10,000) of annual interest from the issuer of the bond since the purchase date. Now, 10 years following the issue date, market interest rates have declined and newly issued bonds similar to the bond you own carry a coupon rate of only 7 percent. Buyers of these new bonds will receive $700 in annual interest (7 percent of the $10,000) compared to the $1,000 annual interest paid by the bond you own. Even though market rates of interest have changed, the coupon rate on your bond is fixed, and your semi-annual interest payments remain unchanged from the date the bond was issued. The bonds you own pay a greater amount of annual interest and will be worth substantially more than newly issued bonds.

The degree to which a bond will sell at a premium or a discount to par value is influenced by the length of time before the bond matures. A bond with a relatively high coupon rate will sell at a larger premium to par value when the bond has a long maturity because above-average interest payments will occur for many years. A bond with an above-market coupon rate is more valuable the longer the time before the bond is scheduled for

Figure 11 ■ Bond Credit Ratings

S&P	Moody's	Fitch	
AAA	Aaa	AAA	High-grade with extremely strong capacity to pay principal and interest
AA	Aa	AA	High-grade by all standards but with slightly lower margins of protection than AAA
A	A	A	Medium-grade with favorable investment attributes but some susceptibility to adverse economic conditions
BBB	Baa	BBB	Medium-grade with adequate capacity to pay interest and principle but possibly lacking certain protection against adverse economic conditions
BB	Ba	BB	Speculative with moderate protection of principal and interest in an unstable economy
B	B	B	Speculative and lacking desirable characteristics of investment bonds. Small assurance principal and interest will be paid on schedule
CCC	Caa	CCC	In default or in danger of default
CC	Ca	CC	Highly speculative and in default or with some other market short-comings
C	C	C	Extremely poor investment quality. Paying no interest
D		D	In default with interest or principal in arrears

redemption. Conversely, a bond with a below-market coupon rate is less valuable the longer the time before the bond is to be redeemed.

The sooner a bond's principal is to be repaid, the more closely the bond will sell to its face value. A $1,000 par value bond that is 1 month from maturity will sell for approximately $1,000 regardless of the bond's coupon rate and the market rate of interest because the face amount of the bond will soon be returned to the bondholder. A bond that is many years from being redeemed may sell at either a large premium or a large discount to its principal amount.

The Risks of Owning Bonds

Bonds are generally less risky to own than common stocks. A bondholder knows exactly how much money to expect and on what dates the money will be received. Compared to a bondholder, a stockholder has less certainty both about dividends and about the future value of the stock. Bondholders are uncertain of the cash payments they will receive only when there is a possibility the bonds may have to be sold prior to maturity or when there is a question about the credit quality of the issuer. Both these uncertainties can be avoided by selecting high-quality bonds with appropriate maturities.

An important risk faced by owners of long-term bonds is the possibility that inflation will eat away at the purchasing power of bond payments. The fixed payments stipulated by bonds hold advantages for a bondholder, but they also create a situation in which persistent inflation will eat away at the real value of each payment. By the time a bond's principal is returned at maturity, a bondholder may find that each dollar received is worth less than 50 cents compared to the dollars originally used to buy the bond. A long period of high inflation may cause bond payments to be worth only pennies on the dollar. The longer a bond's maturity length, the greater the risk that unanticipated inflation will drastically reduce the purchasing power of the bond's interest and principal payments.

Most bonds subject a bondholder to the risk that not all the promised payments will be made by the bond's issuer. Companies that appear to be financially healthy can run into any number of unexpected problems that can leave them unable to service their debt. Times change, and products go out of style at the same time that new competitors attempt to eat away at a firm's market share. Companies will sometimes become overly aggressive in the financing they employ. The 1980s witnessed company after company undertaking substantial borrowing in order to improve the returns earned by their stockholders. In some instances, even healthy companies ended up unable to meet the monumental interest and principal obligations of the added borrowing. Investors who had purchased what was once considered high-quality debt were left holding bonds of questionable value.

Many long-term corporate bonds are subject to early redemption (redemption prior to the scheduled maturity) at a fixed price. Early redemptions are most likely to occur following a period of falling interest rates because borrowers would like to replace their old high-interest debt with newly issued debt at a lower interest rate. The possibility of an early redemption is a serious risk to owners of bonds that can be called away by issuers because the redemption is likely to occur at the worst possible time—a period when the principal returned can be reinvested at a relatively low rate of interest. Before purchasing a bond you should always determine if the bond is subject to early redemption, especially if the bond sells at a premium to par.

Influences on Bond Fund Values

Changes in the net asset values of bond funds result from changes in the market values of the bonds these funds hold in their portfolios. Thus, changes in the NAVs of bond funds are mostly caused by changes in market interest rates. An increase in market interest rates will cause a decline in the net asset values of bond funds because of the decline in the market values of

> **Tip**
>
> The maturity length of a bond fund's portfolio should be a very important consideration in selecting a bond fund to own. Funds that hold portfolios of long-term bonds have net asset values that are heavily influenced by changes in market rates of interest. The net asset values of funds with portfolios of short- and intermediate-term bonds are less affected by interest rate changes.

the bonds these funds are holding. Interest rate changes drive bond values that comprise the portfolios of bond funds.

The extent to which a bond fund's NAV is influenced by changes in interest rates depends on the maturity lengths of the bonds the fund holds in its portfolio. The longer the average maturity of the bonds owned, the more the net asset value of the fund is affected by changing interest rates. Mutual funds that invest in long-term bonds subject their shareholders to a greater variation in share prices than do mutual funds that invest in bonds with intermediate or short maturities. Figure 12 indicates the extent to which maturity length influences a bond's market value at different interest rates. Notice that the price of the 15-year bond is influenced more by interest rate changes than is the bond with a 2-year maturity. The same comparison applies to bond funds that hold long-term bonds in relation to bond funds that hold debt securities with relatively short maturities.

The net asset values of bond funds are affected to a lesser extent by the quality of the bonds owned. A bond fund that holds mostly low-quality bonds (also called *junk bonds*) may experience reductions in NAV during periods of economic decline when investors tend to shy away from risky investments. Some borrowers may cease interest payments during an

Figure 12 ■ Maturity Length and Bond Price Changes

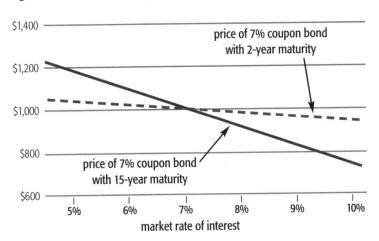

extended period of economic weakness, causing a major decline in the market values of the firms' bonds and substantial erosion in the net asset values of mutual funds that own these bonds.

Types of Bond Funds

Although all bonds are not alike, the variety of bonds is considerably smaller than the variety of common stocks. Bonds differ

> **Tip** It is sometimes wise to consider owning two or three different bond funds, each with a different average maturity length. For example, you might select a fund with long-term bonds, another fund with intermediate-term bonds, and a third fund with short-term bonds. The short-term bond fund provides liquidity at the same time a combination of intermediate- and long-term funds hedge interest rate changes.

mainly by coupon rate, redemption date, credit quality, and type of issuer. With relatively few major differences in all of the thousands of outstanding bond issues, a limited number of factors allow a bond fund to differentiate itself from the thousands of other bond funds in existence.

One important difference among bond funds is the average maturity length of the debt securities held in their portfolios. Bond funds that invest in long-term bonds offer higher current yields and greater NAV volatility compared to bond funds that invest in intermediate-term and short-term bonds. Bond funds that invest in short-term bonds generally offer relatively low current yields but little volatility in NAV. Invest in a mutual fund that holds a portfolio of short-term bonds and you can generally count on being able to liquidate your shares at a price close to what you paid. Keep in mind that that price stability can be either a positive or a negative. It is a positive in a period of rising interest rates and falling bond values but a negative during a period of falling interest rates when long-term bond prices are rising.

Another major differentiating factor is the credit quality of bonds held in a bond fund's portfolio. A bond portfolio of relatively poor credit quality will produce a higher yield from interest compared to a portfolio of high-quality debt, but it will also

Tip Beware of buying shares of a bond fund that offers an unusually high current return. High dividend payments are an indication that a fund may be holding bond issues of low credit quality or bond issues with high coupons selling at a premium to face value. Bonds selling at a premium will eventually be redeemed at face value.

subject owners of the fund to a greater likelihood that a portion of their principal will be lost in defaults, especially in a weak business climate. Still, you may feel that the extra risk is worth the higher current return you will earn from the current income that the fund earns and passes through as dividends.

Bond funds also differ with respect to whether the debt they hold pays tax-exempt interest. Tax-exempt interest paid to a bond fund is passed through to the fund's stockholders as tax-free income, an important consideration for investors who have substantial amounts of taxable income. A large number of mutual funds specialize in owning municipal bonds that pay tax-exempt interest.

The main types of bond funds are:

Corporate bond funds Corporate bond funds invest in debt securities issued and guaranteed by private businesses. These funds pay dividends to shareholders that are taxable by both federal and state authorities. Corporate bond funds generally hold debt of high credit quality but the range of maturities can vary. Funds holding bonds with long maturities tend to offer the highest current yields and have shares that experience the greatest price volatility.

High-yield funds Sometimes called *junk bond funds*, high-yield funds are specialized corporate bond funds that concentrate on owning long-term debt securities that offer unusually high interest income. The high yields are achieved by selecting bonds with low credit ratings and higher-than-average risk of default. These funds often offer substantially higher yields than can be earned from ordinary corporate bond funds. Ownership also entails more risk and the funds can have volatile share values. Dividends received from these funds are normally fully taxable at both the federal and state level.

> **Tip** Bond funds tend to have lower expense ratios than equity funds. Annual expenses are particularly relevant for shareholders of bond funds who are primarily interested in current income rather than capital gains. Expenses of a fund result in a direct reduction in the current income earned by the fund's shareholders.

World bond funds World bond funds invest in debt securities issued and guaranteed by foreign governments and foreign-based companies. These funds attempt to improve stockholder returns by seeking higher yields wherever in the world they are available. Some world bond funds specialize in bonds of a particular region or bonds offered in emerging markets. Returns from owning these funds depend not only on interest income but also on currency exchange rates. Dividends received by shareholders of world bond funds are fully taxable.

Government bond funds Government bond funds invest in U.S. government bonds. Although free of risk from default, government bond funds that concentrate on owning bonds with long maturities tend to have volatile market values. Some of these funds hold bonds with intermediate-term or short-term maturities and have market values that are influenced less by changes in market rates of interest. Dividends received by shareholders of government bond funds are taxable at the federal level but not the state level.

Tax-free bond funds Sometimes called *muni funds*, tax-free bond funds invest in tax-exempt municipal bonds issued by cities, counties, states, and political subdivisions. Many funds specialize in bonds issued in a specific state so that dividends received by a fund shareholder who is also a resident of that particular state is free of both federal and state taxes. Other tax-free bond funds invest in bonds from a range of states. Tax-free bond funds are offered with a wide range of average maturities.

Money market funds Money-market funds invest in short-term debt securities and hold portfolios that must have average maturities of 90 days or less. These funds have a stable share value but pay dividends that fluctuate from month to month and year to year. Many money market funds specialize in short-term municipal debt and pay shareholders dividends that are exempt from federal, and often state, income taxes. Money market funds are discussed more fully in Chapter 5.

5 Money Market Funds

Money market funds are specialized mutual funds that restrict their investments to very short-term debt securities. These funds offer stable share values and excellent liquidity, but only modest yields. Money market funds are particularly useful as substitutes for savings accounts and money market deposit accounts. Although not insured, most money market funds offer a high degree of safety with regard to the principal that is invested. Many funds limit their investments to short-term state and local debt and pay a dividend that is exempt from federal income taxes.

Although money market mutual funds serve a very different investment function compared to equity funds and bond funds that were discussed in chapters 3 and 4, all three types of funds have the same organizational structure. Like equity and bond funds, a money market fund continually issues and redeems shares in response to changes in investor demand. The identifying feature of money market funds is ownership of a portfolio of very short-term debt instruments. Restricting investments to very short-term debt results in these funds having a stable share price (short-term debt instruments do not change much in market value) but relatively low returns. Money market funds have a stable share price because the assets they hold—short-term debt securities—have stable market values. The stable value of the shares, in turn, protects shareholders of money market mutual funds from the major risk of owning equity funds and bond funds: volatility of net asset value.

The Stability of Money Market Fund Share Values

The market values of all negotiable interest-bearing securities are affected to some degree by changing market rates of interest, but securities with maturity lengths of less than a year are affected relatively little. Even large variations in market interest rates have only a small effect on the market values of Treasury bills or negotiable certificates of deposit scheduled to mature in a matter of weeks. A Treasury bill that is scheduled to return its face value of $10,000 in a month can be sold to another investor for very near the face value regardless of the current level of interest rates. Because a mutual fund's net asset value is a direct function of the value of the fund's assets, stable asset values in the fund's portfolio result in a stable net asset value for the fund's shares. Money market securities owned by these funds generally have very active secondary markets and are easily bought and sold without having an effect on their market values. Thus, a money market fund that is subject to large shareholder redemptions can easily liquidate a substantial portion of its portfolio at near to face value in order to raise money to pay for the redeemed shares.

The combination of great liquidity and stable security values enables money market funds to stabilize the net asset value of their shares at $1, thus permitting investors to buy and redeem shares at a fixed price. In other words, as an investor you can purchase shares of a money market fund at $1 per share and later sell the same shares at a price of $1 each. Assets in the fund's portfolio can be readily sold at a known price when

> **Tip** Falling interest rates, not rising interest rates, are a risk for investors who invest in money market funds. Falling interest rates will cause these funds to reduce the yields they provide to their own investors.

shareholders redeem shares, and more securities are easily acquired when a fund receives additional shareholder money. Being able to redeem shares at a fixed value is a shareholder luxury that money market funds, but not equity or bond funds, are able to provide.

Be warned that money market funds do not guarantee that the price of their shares will always be $1. In a few instances, a portion of the investments held by a money market fund have declined in value to such an extent that the fund's managers could not maintain the $1 share price. Rather than suffer the negative publicity that would ensue, the fund sponsors maintained the $1 price by pumping their own money into the fund. This drastic step was not legally required of the sponsors and shareholders could have found themselves holding shares with a value of less than $1. The ability of a fund's managers to maintain a stable share price depends on the maturity length, quality, and liquidity of securities held by the fund. Reaching for higher yields by purchasing securities with longer maturities, lower credit quality, and reduced liquidity can pose risks for shareholders.

Assets Held by Money Market Mutual Funds

Money market funds invest in corporate and government debt securities with very short maturities. The Securities and Exchange Commission requires that these funds maintain portfolios with average maturities of 90 days or less. The average maturity length of a particular fund depends in large part on the portfolio manager's expectation of interest rate changes. A manager who feels short-term rates will be increasing is likely to maintain a portfolio with a relatively short average maturity. Holding securities with short maturities allows the portfolio manager to take advantage of rising interest rates by investing principal at a higher return.

The portfolio of a money market fund is likely to contain Treasury bills, other short-term government securities, repurchase agreements (also called *repos*, these loans use U.S. government securities as collateral), certificates of deposit (CDs) issued by commercial banks and savings and loans, commercial paper (short-term corporate IOUs), and bankers' acceptances (short-term credit instruments guaranteed by commercial banks). Some money market funds also invest in Eurodollar CDs. As a general rule, money market funds restrict their investments to high-quality securities that are easily bought and sold. The Securities and Exchange Commission requires that money market funds invest only in investment-quality commercial paper. The SEC also restricts taxable money market funds from investing more than 5 percent of their assets in the securities of any one issuer. Figure 13 (p. 78) depicts the mix of assets held at the end of 2002 by taxable money market funds.

> **Tip** Annual operating expenses are a particularly important consideration for selecting money market funds that typically offer relatively low yields. Periodically compare the yield for any money market fund you own with similar money market funds from other sponsors.

Figure 13 ■ Asset Mix of a Typical Taxable Money Market Fund

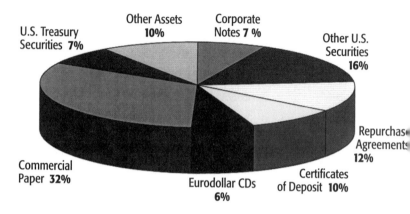

Even though money market funds generally hold high-quality debt instruments, not all the investments purchased by these funds are of equal quality. Just as important is the fact that not all money market funds hold these securities in equal proportion. Money market funds compete for investors primarily via the yields they offer. Funds that provide the highest yields are likely to capture the greatest amount of new investor money. In order to offer higher yields, money market fund portfolio managers sometimes purchase riskier securities that have relatively high yields. Note in Figure 13 the relatively large proportion of commercial paper that offers higher yields but is considered more risky than U.S. Treasury securities. Money market portfolio managers sometimes include securities backed by auto loans and credit-card receivables in their portfolios. A manager may increase the portfolio's yield by including certificates of deposit from financially shaky commercial banks that must pay high interest rates to attract capital. Complicated new securities with floating yields pegged to foreign currencies have also been developed and marketed to money market managers. Likewise, some money market funds are increasingly substituting slightly riskier federal agency issues for direct obligations of the U.S. government. If a borrower defaults on a security held in a money market fund's portfolio, the fund will be stuck with a security of questionable value and the fund's shareholders will observe either a decline in the fund's net asset value or a reduction in the yield.

Types of Money Market Funds

Money market funds are primarily differentiated on the basis of the tax status of the securities held in their portfolios. The majority of money market funds invest in taxable securities, such as short-term U.S Treasury securities and certificates of deposit, and pay taxable dividends to their shareholders. A smaller but increasing number of money market funds invest in short-term tax-exempt debt securities and pay their shareholders tax-exempt dividends (at the federal level). Some money market funds restrict their investments to tax-exempt money market securities from a particular state so that the funds' dividends are exempt from state and local taxes as well as from federal income taxes. Figure 14 (p. 80) illustrates the growth of assets held by taxable and tax-exempt money market funds.

Money market funds that restrict their investments to short-

> **Tip** A money market fund that offers an unusually high yield may have a large proportion of its portfolio in unsecured corporate short-term debt and a small proportion of the portfolio in safer but lower-yielding U.S. government-guaranteed debt securities.

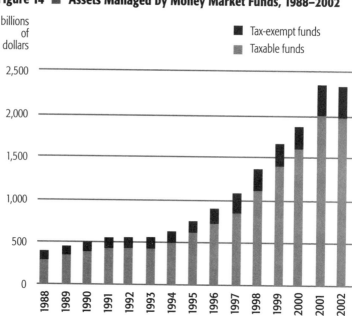

Figure 14 ■ **Assets Managed by Money Market Funds, 1988–2002**

term U.S. government securities gained popularity in the late 1980s and early 1990s when investors became concerned by the increasing number of business bankruptcies and weaknesses in the U.S. financial system. Some funds restrict their investments to direct obligations of the U.S. Treasury in an effort to provide investors with the safest possible portfolio of short-term securities. Investors who reside in states with high income tax rates benefit most from owning money market funds that invest in U.S. government securities because these funds pay dividends that generally escape taxation by state and local authorities (although not the higher rate levied by federal authorities).

Shareholder Expenses Associated with Money Market Funds

Money market funds, even those sold by brokerage firms, do not charge the sales or redemption fees that are common with equity and bond funds. Like these other funds, money market funds do levy an annual fee to cover their operating and portfolio management expenses. Some funds charge as little as 0.3 percent of the fund's average assets annually to pay for operating expenses, while other funds charge nearly twice this rate. Differences in expense ratios among different funds have a direct effect on the yields earned by their shareholders. The differences are especially evident in the yields stockholders receive during periods of low interest rates. When money market funds are earning as little as 1 to 2 percent on short-term debt instruments, an extra annual expense of 0.2 or 0.3 percent makes an important difference in the return a money market shareholder earns.

Some money market funds charge a separate 12b–1 fee to pay for distribution costs, sometimes including payment to salespeople who sell the funds. These fees, which result in a direct reduction in the yield earned by shareholders, are most prevalent among money market funds sold through brokerage firms. It is to your advantage to avoid money market funds that charge a 12b–1 distribution fee. Chapter 6 includes a more complete discussion of charges and fees faced by mutual fund investors.

Tip Yields on money market funds offered by the major brokerage firms are often lower than yields on similar funds offered directly to investors. You can avoid this problem by maintaining a money market account outside and separate from your regular brokerage account.

Utilizing Money Market Funds

Money market funds serve both as a place to temporarily park idle money that you soon expect to use and as a place to keep money that you may require on short notice. For example, a money market fund is useful when you wish to set aside money to pay for an upcoming major expenditure or for an investment you anticipate making. You might place the proceeds from the sale of an investment in a money market fund until other better investments are identified. You can also utilize a money market fund to accumulate savings that will be used within a year or two to pay for expensive purchases such as a new vehicle or major vacation. Money market mutual funds offer flexibility because you can add to your account whenever you like and you can withdraw funds without penalty or taxation whenever the need arises. Withdrawing funds from a money market fund is generally as easy as writing a check. Money market funds are excellent places to stash money for possible emergencies because of the liquidity and safety of principal they offer.

The choice between a taxable or tax-free money market fund can be determined by comparing the after-tax rate of return you will earn from each type of fund. The best choice is a function of both your marginal tax rate and the difference in the yields available on taxable and tax-exempt funds. The smaller the difference between the two yields, the more likely it is that you will benefit from choosing a tax-exempt fund. It is gener-

---

Tip Money market funds offer excellent liquidity and are a good choice for an individual's emergency fund. Assets in an emergency fund should be readily available and have a stable value. Money market funds meet these two requirements.

ally advantageous to stick with a taxable fund unless your federal marginal tax rate is 25 percent or above, although you can be certain only after calculating the after-tax return for each alternative. Determine the after-tax return for a taxable money market fund (or any other investment) using the following formula:

After-tax yield = taxable yield (1 − your marginal tax rate)

For example, if a taxable money market fund is yielding 4 percent and your marginal tax rate is 25 percent, the after-tax return you would earn from owning shares in the fund is:

$$4\% \,(1 - .25) = 4\% \times .75 = 3\%$$

In this case, the 4 percent taxable return provides you with an after-tax return of 3 percent. Thus, it is to your financial advantage to choose a tax-exempt fund only if it yields more than 3 percent. A tax-free return of less than 3 percent means you can earn more from a taxable fund even after paying taxes on the dividends you receive. Residing in a high-tax state such as California or New York may make it desirable to invest in a tax-exempt money market fund that specializes in tax-exempt securities of the state in which you live. In this case, the relative advantage of the tax-exempt fund is greater because you save on state as well as federal income taxes.

When choosing a money market fund keep in mind that yields among these funds can vary so it is worthwhile to investigate a number of funds prior to committing your money. In general, money market funds offered by brokerage firms have higher fees and offer lower yields than funds offered directly by the sponsor. This isn't always the case, but it means you should at least check out yields from several sponsors if you normally maintain a substantial balance in your brokerage account money market fund.

6 Buying and Selling Mutual Funds

Mutual funds utilize several methods to distribute their shares to investors. Most funds sell shares through either a captive or an independent sales force. Other funds choose to sell their shares directly to investors. Purchasing mutual fund shares from a salesperson normally involves some type of sales charge while shares purchased from a fund that sells directly often do not entail either a sales or redemption fee. Money market mutual funds do not charge sales or redemption fees. A mutual fund's fee schedule and the methods it uses to distribute and redeem its shares are spelled out in the fund's prospectus.

If you decide to purchase shares of common stock in Goodyear or you want to acquire $10,000 face amount of bonds issued by the city of Rushville, Indiana, you have little choice but to employ the services of a brokerage firm that will charge a commission when the order is executed. You will also have to go through a brokerage firm and pay a commission to sell bonds or shares of stock that you own. Only a limited number of companies issue their own shares directly to investors, and no firms offer to buy back their shares on demand. All brokerage companies have access to virtually the same wide range of secondary markets.

Mutual fund shares are bought and sold differently than negotiable securities, even though mutual funds are nothing more than corporate shells that hold portfolios of negotiable securities. The shares of many mutual funds are purchased through sales organizations authorized by the funds' sponsors to sell and redeem the shares. Shares of other mutual funds can only be bought from the funds themselves. Mutual funds that operate without the assistance of a sales force must rely on advertising, investment performance, and word of mouth to create investor demand for their shares.

Whether you purchase shares from a salesperson or directly from the fund, the shares you purchase will be issued by the fund and will not come from another investor as is generally the case when you buy individual stocks and bonds. The mutual fund's underwriter issues the shares even when they are purchased through a salesperson. Likewise, shares redeemed through an agent are returned to the fund's underwriter for redemption rather than sold to another investor.

How Mutual Funds Distribute their Shares

A mutual fund employs one of three methods to distribute its shares to investors. Many funds eliminate the need for a sales force by selling their shares directly to the public. These funds appeal to investors who want to avoid dealing with a salesperson and paying a sales commission. Other funds believe a sales force best promotes the funds' interests. Funds that use salespeople to distribute their shares either employ their own sales forces or use the sales staffs of other organizations. Each of the three distribution methods has advantages and disadvantages, both for the fund and for individual investors. A mutual fund's policy regarding the sale and redemption of its shares is spelled out in the fund's prospectus, a legal document that is discussed in greater detail in the following chapter.

Minimum Investment Requirements

Most mutual funds require a minimum initial investment when an account is opened. The minimum varies from one fund to the next, but it is typically $500, $1,000, or $2,500, with bond funds generally requiring larger minimums than stock funds, and funds sold directly requiring higher minimums than funds sold through a sales force. The minimums are often reduced when mutual fund shares are used for a retirement plan or when an investor enters into a contract to make regular purchases. Some funds also establish minimums on subsequent investments to an account, but the required amounts are generally quite small, sometimes only $25 or $50. Figure 15 (p. 88) provides information on the minimum initial investment and minimum subsequent investments for a number of popular mutual funds.

Some mutual funds, including most large funds, offer special programs for share purchases. For example, a mutual fund may offer an accumulation plan in which you agree to periodically purchase shares of the fund. Payment for purchases may be made through payroll deductions or through automatic debiting of your bank account. Some accumulation plans allow substantial flexibility in the amounts you are permitted to invest while other plans involve a firm commitment.

Distribution Through a Sales Force

Many investment companies distribute their shares by establishing sales agreements with independent agents. An insurance agency, a brokerage firm, or a financial planner may serve as an agent for several mutual fund sponsors. Other sponsors distribute their funds through their own sales organizations. Many

Figure 15 ■ Minimum Investments Required by Selected Mutual Funds

Fund	Initial Min.	Subsequent Investment	IRA Min.
Brandywine Fund	$ 25,000	$ 1,000	$25,000
Clipper Fund	5,000	1,000	2,000
Dreyfus Midcap Value Fund	2,500	100	750
FAM Value Fund	500	50	100
Fidelity Global Balanced Fund	2,500	250	500
Gabelli Growth Fund	1,000	100	250
Income Fund of America	250	50	250
Janus Fund	2,500	100	500
Meridian Value Fund	1,000	50	1,000
Nicholas Fund	500	100	500
Oakmark Fund	1,000	100	1,000
Osterweis Fund	100,000	1,000	3,000
Putnam Vista Fund A	500	50	250
Smith Barney Aggressive Growth Fund A	1,000	50	250
Strong Discovery Fund	2,500	100	1,000
Third Avenue Value Fund	1,000	1,000	500
USAA Aggressive Growth Fund	2,000	50	2,000
Vanguard 500 Index Fund	3,000	100	1,000

large insurance companies and brokerage firms that sponsor and manage mutual funds have their own captive sales organizations to distribute the funds. These organizations may also sell the mutual funds of other sponsors.

Not all mutual funds that distribute their shares by means of a sales force can be purchased at every brokerage company or through every sales organization. Each brokerage company, insurance agent, and financial planner handles mutual funds from a limited number of sponsors with which it has sales agreements. However, any sales organization is likely to offer enough variety that you will be able to choose among funds with a wide selection of investment objectives. If you are more interested in choosing a fund with a particular investment objective (e.g., aggressive growth, high current income, or tax-exempt income) than in owning the shares of a particular fund, nearly any broker or financial planner will offer one or more funds that meet your needs. However, if you want to purchase shares of a particular mutual fund, you may have to contact several brokerage firms before you locate one authorized to sell shares of that fund. Alternatively, you can contact the mutual fund and inquire about buying the shares directly or ask what companies are authorized to sell the firm's shares.

Individual brokerage companies sell funds they sponsor through their own sales force. Most large retail broker-dealers sponsor and sell a variety of their own mutual funds as well as funds from other sponsors. Shares of an in-house or proprietary fund can normally only be bought and sold through the firm that sponsors the fund. For example, you can buy and sell the shares of a Merrill Lynch-sponsored fund only through a Merrill Lynch broker. Owning shares of an in-house fund may create a bottleneck if you decide to move your account to a different brokerage firm.

Some sales organizations compensate their salespeople with higher commissions for selling in-house funds compared to the commissions they pay for selling funds from other sponsors. Critics argue that the commission differential can work to an investor's disadvantage because the salesperson has a financial incentive to pitch the firm's products even though an outside sponsor may offer a fund that better fits a customer's needs.

Direct Distribution

Many mutual funds sell their shares directly to the public, thereby avoiding the need either to employ a sales force or to use outside sales organizations. Direct distributors rely heavily on print advertising to attract investors, as a quick inspection of nearly any issue of *The Wall Street Journal*, *Barron's*, or many other financial publications will attest. Direct distributors have toll-free telephone numbers and websites that investors can use to seek information. Direct distributors normally refrain from providing detailed investment advice such as you might expect from a salesperson earning a commission. At the same time, many of the sales representatives you reach by telephone will be knowledgeable concerning the funds they sell, including which funds are most suitable to meet a particular investment objective. Some mutual fund sponsors that sell direct now offer limited investment advice, a topic that is discussed in Chapter 7.

Mutual funds that choose to sell their shares directly cannot normally be purchased through outside sales organizations because the funds offer salespeople no financial incentives. To buy shares from a fund that sells direct, you must call or write the fund and request an application and a prospectus. You can speed the application by utilizing the Internet and visiting the fund's website. These funds generally charge only a small fee, or no fee at all, to buy or redeem their shares. Some discount bro-

> **Tip** If you decide at year-end to sell mutual fund shares in which you have a loss, remember that in order to realize the loss for tax purposes you must wait 30 days before repurchasing shares of the same fund. You can avoid this problem by purchasing shares in a different fund with a similar investment goal.

kerage companies will purchase shares of certain mutual funds for your brokerage account. This arrangement has certain advantages with regard to record keeping and an ability to use shares to collateralize loans.

Distribution Fees You May Have to Pay

If you feel you need counsel concerning what type of mutual fund to buy or if you have decided to invest in a mutual fund that distributes its shares through a sales force, you are likely to be charged some type of fee by the organization that sells the fund. The fee may be assessed when you purchase shares, or it may be deferred until you present the shares for redemption. Some distributors levy a conditional deferred sales charge that declines the longer the shares are owned. A substantial number of mutual funds also levy a distribution fee that is periodically assessed against the fund's assets. Some fund sponsors permit you to choose among two or three different fee schedules for the same mutual fund.

A mutual fund's fees are clearly and concisely presented in the prospectus that is made available to potential investors. The prospectus can be obtained from the fund or a sales agent. It is also generally available online at the sponsor's website. All mutual fund prospectuses present the funds' charges to share-holders in a virtually identical manner, making it relatively easy

Figure 16 ■ An Explanation of Mutual Fund Fees and Expenses

Mutual funds are required to disclose fees in the prospectus. The fee schedule breaks out fees that shareholders will pay when purchasing shares and the fees they will pay during the period shares are owned.

Shareholder Fees

These fees are charged directly to a shareholder when shares are purchased, redeemed, or exchanged

1) *Sales Charge:* A fee attached to the purchase or sale of mutual fund shares that compensates a financial adviser for his or her services.
2) *Redemption Fee:* A fee paid to the mutual fund that is compensation for costs (other than sales costs) incurred from a redemption of shares.
3) *Exchange Fee:* A fee that may be charged when a shareholder transfers money from one fund to another fund within the same family of funds.
4) *Annual Account Maintenance Fee:* A fee that may be charged in order to cover the cost of providing service to an account with a small balance.

Annual Fund Operating Expenses

These fees represent the cost of operating a fund and are deducted from fund assets before earnings are distributed to shareholders.

5) *Management Fee:* A fee charged by the fund's investment adviser for managing the investment portfolio and providing related services.
6) *Distribution Fee (12b–1 Fee):* A charge for marketing and advertising expenses and to compensate sale personnel.
7) *Other Expenses:* Miscellaneous expenses including phone bills, account services, website maintenance, postage, and payments to the transfer agent.

---

to compare the fees charged by various funds. A prospectus divides fees into two sections: (1) transaction expenses charged only once during the time a shareholder owns shares in the fund, and (2) annual operating expenses that are charged against the fund's income each year. Fee tables sometimes include all categories of potential fees even though a particular fund may not levy some of the fees. Figure 16 provides a summary list and explanation of the fees you may be required to pay as a mutual fund shareholder. Fees in the first group are paid directly while fees included as annual fund operating expenses are paid indirectly through reduced earnings distributions by the fund.

Front-End Load Charges

Until the early 1970s sales agents sold the majority of mutual funds and received compensation from a sales charge paid by the investors who purchased shares. The charge, also called a *load*, ranged up to 8.5 percent of the money a customer invested. If you invested $5,000 in one of these funds, a front-end load of $425 (8.5 percent of your $5,000 investment) was immediately deducted to compensate the salesperson and distributor. After deduction of the distribution fee, only $4,575 of the original $5,000 investment was available to purchase shares of the fund. The 8.5 percent sales fee actually amounted to 9.3 percent of the money that went to purchase shares in the fund ($425/$4,575). On the positive side, the era of 8.5 percent loads did not include additional charges for share redemptions.

Money market funds without a sales fee were first offered to investors in the early 1970s. The spectacular success of these funds, combined with an exodus of individuals from the securities markets in general and mutual funds in particular, convinced a number of mutual fund sponsors to bypass their regular sales channels, drop the sales charges, and sell their funds directly to investors. Mutual funds sold without a sales fee (*no-load funds*) had been around for many years prior to the 1970s, but not on a major scale.

The success of mutual fund sponsors that switched to direct distribution of their shares helped initiate several important changes in the industry. To compete with the no-loads, some mutual fund sponsors dropped their sales fees and instead charged a redemption fee. These funds merely moved the charge from the opening transaction to the closing transaction, partly so that salespeople could tell potential customers that no fees were being charged when shares were purchased. "Every dollar you invest will be used to buy shares in the fund," they would note, while glossing over the "redemption surprise." Other funds reduced the size of their sales fee in order to compete with funds sold directly to investors.

Competition among an exploding number of mutual funds has caused a general reduction in the percentage sales fees that most funds charge. Equity funds sold through brokers, insurance agents, and financial planners typically charge fees that range from 4 to 6.5 percent of the amount invested. Bond funds sold through sales organizations generally have sales fees of 3 to 5 percent of the amount invested.

Many mutual fund sponsors that levy a front-end sales fee reduce the fee for large purchases. For example, one large fund charges a 5 percent sales fee for an investor's purchases up to $25,000; 4.25 percent on purchases of $25,001 to $100,000; 3.25 percent on purchases of $100,001 to $500,000; and 2.00 percent on investments above $500,000. Both the loads and the amounts that must be invested to benefit from a reduction in the loads vary from fund to fund.

In an unusual twist, the renewed popularity of mutual funds during the 1980s bull market in both stocks and bonds caused some no-load funds to begin charging sales fees, not to pay a salesperson but to provide the mutual funds with an additional source of revenue that was used to attract new investors. The fees initiated by the former no-loads were generally small, often 3 percent or less, thereby earning a new fee classification, *low-load funds*.

Among the funds that charge a load, fees tend to be higher

for equity funds than for bond funds, and among stock funds, fees are generally higher for specialized funds that have a relatively small market and are likely to be difficult for a salesperson to explain to potential investors. Many specialized funds are subject to substantial price volatility that attracts investors who are more interested in performance than in saving 1 or 2 percent in sales fees.

Some funds that have a front-end load also charge a sales fee on reinvested dividends and capital gains distributions. This expense applies only if you have elected to reinvest your distributions in additional shares of a fund's stock. Fortunately, funds that levy this fee are the exception rather than the rule.

Redemption Fees and Back-End Loads

Redemption fees and back-end loads (also called *deferred sales charges*) are paid when shares are redeemed rather than when shares are purchased. Redemption fees generally go to compensate the mutual fund for the expense of servicing the account and taking care of the redemption while back-end loads compensate brokers. Both charges have the effect of reducing the amount of money a shareholder receives when shares are sold. Many mutual fund sponsors have substituted redemption fees for front-end loads because they believe the deferred fees are more palatable to investors, thus making the funds easier to sell.

> **Tip** It is generally best to avoid purchasing mutual fund shares near the end of the year just prior to capital gains distributions. Buying just prior to a distribution causes you to incur a tax liability on the distribution even though the distribution will be offset by a decline in the net asset value of the shares.

Figure 17 ■ Effect of Front-End Load vs. Deferred Sales Charge

	Fund with Front-End Load	Fund with Deferred Sales Charge
Amount invested	$10,000	$10,000
Front-end load (4%)	400	0
Net investment	$ 9,600	$10,000
Value of net investment in 10 years assuming 7% average annual growth	$18,885	$19,672
Deferred sales charge (4%)*	0	787
Net proceeds	$18,885	$18,885

*Assumes deferred sales is based on redemption value rather than purchase price. Also assumes the deferred charge is not reduced according to the length of the holding period.

The swelling federal deficit and mountains of personal debt serve as monuments to the willingness of the American people to put off the pain of paying for anything.

Some funds, including many sponsored by brokerage companies, levy a *contingent deferred sales charge* based on the length of time the shares have been held prior to being redeemed. For example, a fund might charge a 6 percent fee when shares have been held less than a year, 5 percent when shares have been held more than one year but less than two years, 4 percent when shares have been held more than two years but less than three, and so forth. Using this particular fee schedule allows a shareholder to escape a deferred sales charge if shares are held six years or more. A contingent deferred sales charge guarantees a minimum return to the sponsor either from annual expense charges (if you remain in the fund) or the deferred sales charge (if you hold the shares for less than six years). The contingent fee is appealing to investors who are offered an opportunity to purchase mutual fund shares without paying a sales fee. A contingent deferred sales charge is generally based on the lesser of either your initial investment or the value of your shares at the time of the redemption.

Does it really make any difference whether you are charged a 4 percent front-end load or a 4 percent redemption fee? Suppose you invest $10,000 in a front-end load fund that annually increases in value by 7 percent for 10 years, at which time you redeem the shares. Figure 17 illustrates that your $9,600 net investment ($10,000 less the $400 initial sales charge) will increase in 10 years to $18,885 if the fund averages a 7 percent annual return. Now suppose the fund charges a 4 percent redemption fee on the proceeds rather than a 4 percent front-end load. Your $10,000 investment will amount to $19,672 at the end of 10 years, but you will be required to pay a deferred sales fee equal to 4 percent of the terminal value, or $787, leaving $18,885, the same amount calculated with the 4 percent front-end load. This example assumes that the deferred sales charge is calculated on the value of the shares that are redeemed rather than the initial cost. If the redemption fee had been based on the initial purchase price, the comparison would favor the redemption fee over the front-end load assuming the fund earns a positive return.

> **Tip**
>
> When redeeming shares that have been purchased on different dates at different prices, you may want to specify which shares are being redeemed. For example, you may wish to sell the shares for which you paid the highest price in order to reduce your capital gain and the tax you will be required to pay. Identifying shares is only an issue if you are redeeming only a portion of the shares you own.

Annual Fees to Cover Selling Expenses

Some mutual funds cover all or a portion of their sales and marketing expenses, sometimes including payments to salespeople, by charging a fee calculated as a percentage of the average daily assets being managed. For example, a fund may establish an annual charge equal to .25 percent of the fund's average daily assets. The charge, called a *12b–1 fee* after the 1980 SEC rule that permits investment companies to assess the fee, is sometimes used in place of a front-end load or a deferred sales charge, or it may be charged in addition to one or both of these other fees. The SEC does not limit the size of 12b–1 fees but NASD rules require that the fee used to cover marketing and distribution expenses cannot exceed .75 percent. An additional 12b–1 fee of .25 percent is permitted to cover "shareholder services." Although the fee is relatively small, the recurring charge causes a long-term investor to incur substantial costs over the course of many years. The SEC's intent in allowing a 12b–1 fee was to provide mutual funds with the financial resources to attract new investors, thus increasing the amount of assets managed by the funds that would permit the funds to achieve economies of scale and reduce their expense ratios.

Annual fees used to pay mutual fund marketing expenses were initially called *hidden loads* because the charges were buried among other annual expenses. Thus, a mutual fund could trim its front-end or back-end load and initiate a 12b–1 fee to more effectively compete for the money of investors who sought to avoid sales and redemption fees. In reality, a relatively modest annual fee can prove more expensive to an investor than either a front-end load or a redemption fee.

A .75 percent (.75 of 1 percent) annual 12b–1 fee reduces the return you will earn by .75 percent for each year the mutual fund is owned. The continuing expense eventually will cause this cumulative fee to be more costly than either a front-end load or a back-end load if you own a mutual fund for many years. Figure 18 compares the effects of a .75 percent annual 12b–1 fee and a 4 percent one-time front-end load for 10 years on a $10,000 investment. The chart assumes an annual return of 7 percent (reduced to 6.25 percent for the 12b–1 fund). An investment in the fund with the 4 percent load is initially worth less than the same investment in the fund with the 12b–1 fee ($9,600 vs. $10,000), but by the end of the sixth year the value of the fund with the front-end load has slightly surpassed the value of the fund with the 12b–1 fee. From that point on the gap between the 2 funds increases until by the tenth year the fund with the load has a value of $18,885 while the fund with the 12b–1 fee has a value of $18,335.

Figure 18 ■ Comparing Front-End Sales Fee with Annual 12b-1 Fee

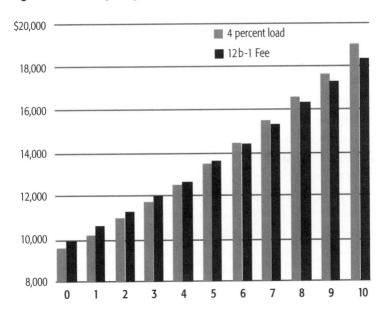

Figure 19 ■ Fees Charged by Selected Mutual Funds

Fund	Max. Load	12b–1 Fee	Exp. Ratio	1st Yr Red. Fee
APX New Dimensions Fund	5.75%	.25%	1.06%	0%
Fidelity Global Balanced Fund	0	0	1.25	0
Fidelity Magellan Fund	3.00	0	.89	0
Gabelli Growth Fund	0	.25	1.40	0
INVESCO Dynamics Fund	0	.25	1.21	0
Janus Fund	0	0	.84	0
Osterweis Fund	0	0	1.42	2.0
Putnam Vista Fund A	5.75	.25	.89	0
Scudder Growth Fund	5.75	.24	1.03	0
Smith Barney Aggressive Growth A	5.00	.25	1.21	0
Vanguard 500 Index Fund	0	0	.18	0

Some mutual fund sponsors allow investors to choose among several fee structures for the same fund. For example, one large mutual fund offers investors a choice of buying Class A shares and paying a maximum 6.5 percent front-end load (reduced for purchases exceeding $10,000) or of buying Class B shares and paying an annual 1 percent 12b–1 fee along with a contingent deferred sales charge of up to 4 percent. The Class B shares have no front-end sales charge. The contingent sales charge, based on the original cost of the shares, is reduced by 1 percent for each year the fund is held. You would be better served by selecting the Class A shares and avoiding the higher annual expense if you planned to hold the shares for an extended period. Figure 19 illustrates the fees charged by several popular mutual funds.

Evaluating Distribution Fees

Distribution fees should be an important consideration when you choose a mutual fund. If you have a relatively good understanding of your own investment needs, how mutual funds operate, the importance of funds' investment objectives, and what type of investment objectives best meet your needs, you may want to select among mutual funds with no front- or back-end loads and no 12b–1 fees. On the other hand, if you are unsure not only about what particular fund to choose, but even what type of fund you should own, a reasonable distribution charge may be money well spent if the person selling the fund can provide you with worthwhile investment advice. Keep in mind that a larger fee does not necessarily mean you will receive better advice.

Be certain to examine a mutual fund's expense ratio at the same time you evaluate distribution costs. A fund may keep its distribution fees low but impose relatively high annual charges to cover operating expenses. Some studies indicate that a mutual fund with a reasonable front-end load can actually produce better results than no-load funds over long periods of time

> **Tip** The 12b–1 fee is named after a 1980 ruling by the Securities and Exchange Commission. The fee, which can range to a maximum of 0.75 percent of average net assets per year, is designed to cover distribution expenses such as advertising, general market costs, and brokers' commissions.

because funds with a sales charge tend to have smaller expense ratios. This is a generalization, of course, and it is important that you consider all the costs of investing in a particular fund. Fortunately, the mutual fund prospectus and the mutual fund advisory services discussed in Chapter 9 significantly ease the task of making cost comparisons.

7 Selecting a Mutual Fund

Before committing your money to a mutual fund, you should first determine what you expect from your investments. Defining your own financial goals will assist in selecting mutual funds with investment objectives that are compatible with your needs. The diversification and professional management provided by a mutual fund do not eliminate the risks of investing. The prospectus provided by a mutual fund is one of the best sources of information about the fees, investment objectives, and past performance of the fund.

With nearly 8,000 mutual funds ready and willing to accept your money, it is not a simple task to determine which fund or funds is the best choice. Should you choose a fund that sells its shares directly, thereby saving a sales or redemption fee? Should you trust your broker and invest in the mutual funds he or she recommends even though the purchase will entail a sales or redemption charge? Should you buy into a fund based mostly on last year's investment performance, or should you be concerned more about a fund's long-term performance? How important is a mutual fund's expense ratio? Should you search for a fund with a relatively stable net asset value, or do you have to accept price variations in order to have a chance to earn substantial capital gains? These are only a few of the many questions you should answer before selecting a mutual fund.

Identifying Your Investment Goals

Unless you are unusually wealthy, you will never be able to acquire or achieve everything that you desire: exotic vacations, a new vehicle each year, jewelry, early retirement, private schools for your children who will then move on to a "name" college. The list is limited only by your imagination. Unfortunately, limited financial resources are likely to keep you from achieving every goal, including some that you consider quite important. Without a system to prioritize your goals, you are likely to spend your limited financial resources on many things that you deem fairly unimportant, causing you to miss out on some goals that you consider crucial. How many times have you impulsively spent money on something of questionable value and later wished you had the money back because you were unable to afford something else?

It may seem farfetched to believe people would spend money on things that are not high on their wish list, but how many people do you know who buy whatever happens to present itself first? They see new clothes and buy them. A new appliance? No problem. Whatever comes down the pike first consumes their income and depletes their savings. Lack of a spending plan causes these individuals to sacrifice their long-term goals simply because they occur later, after all the money has been consumed by earlier purchases.

This is not the way you lead your own life, of course. You are more thoughtful and deliberate. So how much financial assistance will you be able to provide for your children's college education? When will you be able to afford a comfortable retirement? How frequently should you be trading automobiles? To get a handle on answers to these and other questions that are important to your financial health, you should draw up a list of your goals and—this is the difficult part—determine which of these goals are most important to you and your family. The goals you establish and when you want to achieve them each play a major part in selecting appropriate mutual funds.

The process of establishing and evaluating financial goals is important but somewhat afield for an introductory book on mutual funds. The long and short of it is that you need to estimate the cost and approximate date for each of your major financial goals. When do you want to retire and what size retirement fund will you need? When will your children be ready for college and how much will four years of education cost? When do you plan to trade vehicles and what is an estimate of the cost? If trading vehicles every two or three years and accumulating an adequate college fund are unlikely to both be achieved, which is more important? The funds you need to accumulate and the date the funds are required are major determinants of the types of mutual funds you should choose to own.

Matching Mutual Funds with Your Financial Goals

It is important to choose mutual funds with investment objectives that are compatible with your goals. If you are in your twenties and interested in an early start on a retirement fund, you will be interested in a mutual fund that emphasizes capital growth rather than current income or liquidity. Electing to go

---

Tip The most important rule of mutual fund investing is to select funds with investment goals that are similar to your own goals. Aggressive growth funds are appropriate for some investors but not for others. Likewise, mutual funds that concentrate on current income are not appropriate for all investors.

with an equity fund whose investment objective is capital growth eliminates the majority of mutual funds from consideration. At the opposite end of the investment spectrum, equity funds and long-term bond funds are not appropriate investment tools to serve as an emergency fund where safety, stability, and liquidity are important requirements.

Choosing Funds with Appropriate Investment Horizons

Rather than selecting a separate mutual fund to serve as an investment vehicle for each goal you have identified, you should attempt to realize your goals by pursuing an overall investment strategy. Are your goals heavily weighted toward the long-term (as would be the case for retirement or eventual college financial assistance for young children)? If so, you should concentrate your investments in mutual funds that have long-term investment objectives. On the other hand, if you are mostly concerned about current income, you need to concentrate your investments in mutual funds with portfolios of bonds or income stocks.

Most individuals have a combination of goals that require a blended portfolio of several mutual funds. You are likely to be best served by owning shares in three types of funds: a money market fund, an intermediate- or long-term bond fund, and an equity fund. The money market fund provides stability and liquidity to take care of emergencies and other immediate needs, the bond fund provides current dividends to supplement your other income, and the equity fund provides (hopefully) capital appreciation that will help achieve your long-term goals. It is generally bad investment policy to consign all your savings to a single fund or to several funds with a similar investment objective.

Whether you choose to invest in an aggressive equity fund or a more conservative equity fund depends primarily on your risk tolerance and the goals you have identified. If you consider a goal to be particularly important and feel that it can be achieved without taking high risks, it is best to settle for a conservative fund that is less likely to exhibit large price swings. On the other hand, if you will only be able to achieve a certain goal by earning a very high rate of return, you may decide on an all-or-nothing investment and choose an aggressive growth fund.

Suppose you estimate that in monetary terms your goals are 60 percent long-term, 25 percent intermediate-term, and 15 percent short-term. You should go about establishing a mutual fund portfolio that is compatible with this mix of goals. Another investor who has goals and monetary requirements that are different from your own is likely to benefit most from a different portfolio of mutual funds. Long-term personal financial goals are best met with mutual funds that have long-term investment goals while short-term personal financial needs are best met with mutual funds that strive for current income, stability of value, liquidity, and safety of principal. Figure 20 (p. 108) provides an illustration of sample portfolios for individuals or couples with different investment objectives. The more conservative portfolio for a couple nearing retirement is more heavily weighted with bond funds and money market funds. Bond funds provide a relatively high level of current income while money market funds offer the ultimate in liquidity. Retired individuals will also want to hold a portion of their assets in equity funds that provide some protection against inflation. Still, older investors should generally concentrate on investments that provide current income, liquidity, and stability of value. The sample portfolio for a young couple is more aggressive with a large investment position in equities including growth stocks that are risky and blue chip stocks that offer more stability of value. Both types of equities offer the potential for earning a high return.

Figure 20 ■ Sample Mutual Fund Portfolios for Changing Investment Needs

	Young Couple	Mid-Career Couple	Nearing Retirement
Cash (Money Market Fund)	15%	10%	15%
Intermediate Bonds (Bond Fund)	0	15	20
Long-Term Bonds (Bond Fund)	15	20	40
Growth Stocks (Small-Cap Fund)	35	15	5
Blue Chip Stocks (Large-Cap Fund)	25	30	15
Foreign Stocks (Foreign Equity Fund)	10	10	5

Consider that individuals in their twenties and thirties can expect an extended period of employment that will allow time to recover from occasional sharp declines in stock prices. Individuals near or already in retirement do not enjoy this luxury and a significant loss of principal can prove to be devastating. Many middle age and older individuals lost substantial sums of money from investments in technology stocks during the major market decline that commenced in 2001. Keep in mind that age is important but certainly not the only factor in assembling an investment portfolio. Thus, the sample portfolios of Figure 20 are not appropriate for every couple in each age category. A retired couple with substantial pension income may want a larger proportion of assets in equities, especially if there is an intention to leave a substantial estate to children or charity.

Established goals should be continuously reevaluated. Growing older and achieving certain goals while forgoing others means you are likely to want to revise the goals that remain. A revision of your goals is likely to mean you should consider reallocating your existing mutual fund investments. For example, once you successfully establish an emergency fund, you may want to concentrate a larger proportion of your subsequent investments in mutual funds that have long-term investment objectives. Likewise, closing in on retirement means you should consider moving money out of growth funds and into income funds that provide higher current income and greater stability. The mix of your investment portfolio is known as *asset allocation*. Altering the mix of investments is more convenient if you own mutual funds that are part of a family of funds. This allows you to reallocate your investment among the various available funds.

Choosing Funds with Appropriate Risk Characteristics

Mutual funds are not all equally risky. Some funds own securities that have very volatile market prices. A mutual fund that invests in stocks with volatile market prices will have a volatile net asset value because stocks tend to rise and fall in price together. If you invest in a mutual fund that owns volatile stocks and suddenly discover that you need to sell your shares, you may realize a large loss in value. Of course, it is also possible that you will sell your shares for a large profit, but the uncertainty of not knowing how much you will receive for your shares makes the shares risky to own. It isn't necessarily wrong to invest in a mutual fund that has

Tip   Buying shares in a mutual fund that is part of a family of funds makes it easier to move money between funds. Most sponsors that offer a large number of different mutual funds charge only a nominal fee when their shareholders liquidate shares in one fund and move the proceeds to another fund.

a volatile net asset value, of course, if the fund meets your investment needs and you can tolerate the risks.

Mutual funds that invest in long-term government or corporate bonds are subject to major changes in net asset value whenever long-term interest rates change. A large increase in long-term interest rates will cause a substantial decline in the net asset value of a long-term bond fund. You must decide if the higher current return from a long-term bond fund (long-term bonds normally pay higher interest income than intermediate- or short-term bonds) is worth the added volatility of the fund's net asset value. If there is a likelihood that you will have to sell your shares on short notice, you should probably consider buying shares in an intermediate-term bond fund rather than a long-term bond fund because intermediate-term bonds experience smaller changes in value compared to long-term bonds.

A major consideration in determining your risk tolerance is the importance you attach to the goals you are attempting to achieve. The more important the goal, the less tolerance you have for risky investments. For example, you may have certain goals that you simply must achieve. Suppose you are nearing retirement and have been putting aside money to supplement your social security and employer-sponsored pension. If this supplemental income will be critical to your financial well-being, you will want to move your investment funds to a mutual fund that provides high current income but with great safety of principal. You should not trust all of your retirement money to an equity fund or a mutual fund that invests in high-yield, high-risk bonds. Rather, you should choose a fund that invests in high-grade corporate securities or U.S. government securities. In truth, you may want to hedge your bets and invest in two funds with similar investment objectives.

If there is some possibility that your living expenses will

> **Tip** A broker is unlikely to promote a mutual fund that he or she doesn't sell. Thus, buying a mutual fund through a broker means you are unlikely to learn about mutual funds that may offer better performance, lower expenses, and no sales fee.

require all of your investment income and a portion of your investment principal (i.e., require that you periodically sell some of your mutual fund shares), the stability of the net asset value of your shares becomes a very important consideration. The problem you face is that mutual funds with stable NAVs typically provide fairly modest returns. A solution may be to keep a portion of your savings in a money market fund or a short-term bond fund at the same time that you maintain a position in one or more income funds.

Buying Directly vs. Buying from a Salesperson

The previous chapter discussed the differences between buying mutual funds directly and buying mutual funds through a broker, insurance agent, or financial planner. Buying funds directly will reduce or eliminate sales and redemption fees, although you must generally give up the advice to which you are entitled when you buy shares through a broker or financial planner. If you know so little about investing that you have no idea what type of mutual fund (aggressive growth fund, bond fund, or money market fund) to buy, you should probably bite the bullet and purchase shares from a salesperson who can and will provide investment advice. If you choose this option, you should keep in mind that the salesperson has a vested interest in making his or her investment product look as good as possible.

You are more than halfway home if you have sorted through

your financial goals and understand your financial situation well enough so that you feel comfortable determining the types of mutual funds you should buy. A number of information sources can assist you in selecting individual funds within categories. A select group of these sources is discussed in Chapter 9. Some sources provide substantial detail including historical returns, expenses, and ratings. Of course, if you rely on these publications to assist you in selecting mutual funds, you must be willing to spend time conducting your own research. Time and effort are the prices you must pay for going it alone.

Free or low-cost investment advice has recently opened up for mutual fund investors. A few mutual funds that sell directly are now offering limited investment advice. In 1991, Dreyfus Corporation started providing free asset-allocation advice to individual investors. The company provides a recommended mix of bonds, stocks, and money-market investments based on financial information supplied on a Dreyfus questionnaire by individual investors. In late 1992, Fidelity Investments announced a new program that offered to recommend a mix of Fidelity mutual funds to best meet an individual's particular needs. The recommendation is based on information you supply on a Fidelity questionnaire. Fidelity also operates an advisory service that offers to manage individual portfolios of mutual funds for a maximum fee, the size of which is based on the assets you own. The service requires a minimum portfolio value.

Selecting Funds on the Basis of Past Performance

Investors who feel comfortable selecting mutual funds without the aid of a salesperson are likely to be influenced by the funds' historical investment performance. Even investors who follow

> **Tip** Unusually good investment performance by a mutual fund is often the result of the fund holding a specialized portfolio. Specialized portfolios tend to exhibit large variations in value, both up and down, which means these funds tend to be risky to own.

the recommendation of an investment advisor are usually swayed by the returns a fund has earned for its shareholders. Americans may have a proud history of rooting for the underdog, but most mutual fund investors prefer to put their money in funds that have a record of superior investment performance. So is past performance a good guide to future performance? Should you select a mutual fund based primarily on the fund's historical returns?

Evaluating mutual funds on the basis of the returns they have earned for investors in years past requires an adjustment for risk. Financial theorists believe that accepting greater risks tends to produce greater returns over a long period of time. Thus, mutual funds such as aggressive growth funds or junk bond funds that own securities that entail substantial risk will, over time, provide investors with superior investment returns. Over many years common stock funds should earn higher returns than corporate bond funds, and corporate bond funds should earn higher returns than government bond funds. These relationships do not hold true during every month, during every year, or even over every period of several years. Over the long haul, however, the evidence supports the linkage between risk and return.

Hundreds of tests evaluating mutual fund performance have been undertaken, and the majority of these tests indicate the following:

1. Mutual fund managements have difficulty earning a risk-adjusted return that is superior to the return that can be earned from a naïve buy-and-hold strategy.

2. Sales and redemption charges and expense ratios are important in explaining the differences in risk-adjusted returns among mutual funds. This connection indicates that you should make your choices among funds that have low expenses and modest or no sales and redemption charges.

3. Short-term investment performance is not a good indicator of how a mutual fund will perform in future periods. Don't select a mutual fund based on the fund's return during the past six months or the past year.

4. If a mutual fund's historical returns over a longer period of time are to be an important decision criterion, make certain to determine if the fund's management has recently changed. Good management can quickly turn into mediocre management when the superior talent goes elsewhere.

5. Mutual fund managements tend to have difficulty timing the market. That is, professional portfolio managers are generally unable to forecast overall market movements or movements in particular sectors on any kind of consistent basis. This means you should beware of buying mutual funds that

Tip

Mutual fund sponsors typically offer a reduced sales commission rate for large purchases. These reductions may apply to purchases over time or to cumulative purchases by different family members. A 2003 SEC study indicated that investors are often not credited with the reduced commissions they deserve. Always ask the salesperson if you are eligible for a reduced sales commission.

have unusually large portfolio turnovers. Extensive trading is likely to increase costs and decrease investor returns.

The Advantages of Dollar-Cost Averaging

Although not a technique for selecting mutual funds, dollar-cost averaging is a worthwhile investment technique that is easily applied to mutual fund investing. Dollar-cost averaging is nothing new, and the methodology is easy to understand and implement.

If professional portfolio managers have difficulty choosing the best time to invest, there is no reason to believe that individual investors can do any better. Many financial advisors suggest that individuals are best served by *dollar-cost averaging*, the investment technique of investing a constant amount of money at regular intervals. Dollar-cost averaging requires that you invest equal amounts of money each month or each quarter regardless of how the market has been performing and regardless of what you expect the market to do in future months. Rather than attempt to outguess the market and invest only when you forecast rising stock prices or rising bond prices, it is best to forge ahead and build your mutual fund portfolio period by period without regard to actual or expected near-term price movements. The success of dollar-cost averaging depends on the market increasing over the long term.

Individual investors often become discouraged and quit investing (or sell existing investments) during the latter stages of a major decline in security prices. People throw in the towel because they get tired of losing money. Thus, individual investors often exit the market when stock prices are relatively low and a moderate investment could purchase a relatively large number of mutual fund shares. Likewise, individuals often become exceedingly confident and commit large sums of money to investments during the latter stages of a bull market. Buying stock in a rising market means a given amount of money purchases fewer and fewer shares. Committing to a program of dollar-cost averaging avoids these traps. Dollar-cost averaging results in buying a larger number of shares when prices have declined. The lower the net asset value of a mutual fund's shares, the greater the number of shares you are able to purchase each period. A rising market causes you to purchase fewer shares each period with the same dollar investment.

Figure 21 illustrates the investment record for a person who has implemented a dollar-cost averaging investment program over a four-year period. This investor has decided to invest equal amounts of money each quarter of the year. During the first two years, the individual invested $500 per quarter in the shares of a mutual fund. This investment increased to $600 per quarter in the following two years. The investor is able to purchase 46.512 shares of the mutual fund in the first quarter when the net asset value is $10.75. In the last quarter of 2002, when the offering price has risen to $12.50, $500 buys only 40 shares of the fund. The far right column shows the average price paid for all the shares held up to that point.

An investment program of dollar-cost averaging does not dictate that you always maintain exactly the same periodic investment. An increase in income may cause you to occasionally increase the amount of your monthly or quarterly investment. You should never alter the amount of your investment because of a change in your assessment of the market. Dollar-cost averaging takes out of your hands the decision of how much and when to invest at the same time it requires the discipline to continue investing in the face of an occasionally discouraging market.

Dollar-cost averaging can be applied to simultaneous invest-

Figure 21 ■ Example of Dollar-Cost Averaging

Year	Quarter	Amount Invested	Purchase Price/Sh.	Shares Purchased	Shares Owned	Average Price
2001	I	$500	$10.75	46.512	46.512	$10.75
	II	500	11.25	44.444	90.956	10.99
	III	500	12.00	41.667	132.623	11.31
	IV	500	11.00	45.455	178.078	11.23
2002	I	500	11.50	43.478	221.556	11.28
	II	500	11.75	42.553	264.109	11.36
	III	500	12.25	40.816	304.925	11.48
	IV	500	12.50	40.000	344.925	11.60
2003	I	600	12.75	47.059	391.984	11.74
	II	600	13.00	46.154	438.138	11.87
	III	600	12.75	47.059	485.197	11.95
	IV	600	13.00	46.154	531.351	12.04
2004	I	600	13.50	44.444	575.795	12.15
	II	600	13.25	45.283	621.078	12.24
	III	600	12.75	47.059	668.137	12.27
	IV	600	13.00	46.154	714.291	12.32
Total amount invested			$ 8,800			
Portfolio value after four years			$ 9,864			

ments in different mutual funds. Suppose you determine that you will invest $1,000 each quarter. Depending upon your goals and financial circumstances, you might decide on a quarterly investment of $600 in a stock growth fund, $250 in an inter-mediate-term bond fund, and $150 in a money market fund. Changing the allocation of your investments among these funds would be compatible with dollar-cost averaging so long as you made changes in response to changes in your financial needs rather than to changes in the market.

> **Tip** Try to avoid owning mutual funds that charge a 12b–1 fee. These fees are designed to cover distribution expenses and have nothing to do with improving a mutual fund's investment performance. In fact, the fee comes directly out of the return earned by the fund.

Importance of the Prospectus

The first order of business when you consider an investment in a mutual fund is research. First determine the type of fund or funds in which you should invest. This is a crucial part of the decision. After determining which category of fund is best suited to your needs, obtain and study the prospectus for each fund you might consider choosing. Mutual funds do not charge to mail a copy of these documents but you are likely to find it quicker and easier to check the sponsor's website and view the prospectus online. Never, never, never buy the shares of a mutual fund without first reading the fund's prospectus. Even though the document contains legal jargon that is sometimes difficult to interpret, enough valuable and understandable information is contained in a prospectus to make it worth your time to carefully review this important document before investing your money. A prospectus bares a mutual fund's soul to anyone who is interested enough to take a peek. In particular you should look for these items:

The fund's investment objective Is the fund's goal to maximize dividend income, maximize interest income, earn short-term gains, seek long-term capital growth, provide a stable share price, or earn tax-exempt income? The answer is crucial in determining whether the fund can best serve your financial requirements. Does the fund meet its stated objective by investing in short-term municipal securities, common stocks, long-term corporate bonds, or intermediate-term government bonds? Does the fund's management plan cause it to engage in frequent trading? A mutual fund's investment objective is a major determinant of the types of securities held in the fund's portfolio and of the risks you will face as a shareholder of the fund. It is very important that you select a fund whose investment goal is compatible with your own financial objectives.

The fees charged and the impact of these fees on your investment in the fund Because mutual funds can levy several different types of fees, it is important that you understand the charges you will pay if you purchase shares in the fund. Not all mutual funds charge the same types of fees or the same level of fees. The fund's fees and the effect of these fees are described in the first section of the prospectus.

The method of purchasing and redeeming shares of the fund A section of Chapter 6 described several methods used by mutual funds to distribute their shares to investors. The prospectus will explain if the fund allows you to purchase shares directly or whether you must go through an outside salesperson. It will also describe how the fund's shares can be redeemed.

A financial statement illustrating the per-share income and capital changes during the ten previous years The historical financial statement provides a look at the fund's past investment performance, thus allowing you to compare the performance of competing funds. The financial statement details annual income, expenses, investment income, dividends, gains on investments, and changes in net asset value. A financial statement found in a mutual fund prospectus is illustrated in Figure 22 (p. 120).

Figure 22 ■ Financial Statement from a Mutual Fund Prospectus
(Year Ended January 31)

Net asset value, beginning of year	2002	2001	2000	1999	1998
	$5.24	**$7.22**	**$7.45**	**$8.66**	**$8.21**
Income from investment operations:					
Net investment income	.49(1)	.66	.73	.78	.72
Net gains or losses on securities (both realized and unrealized)	(.50)(1)	(1.98)	(.23)	(1.21)	.45
Total from investment operations	(.01)	(1.32)	.50	(.43)	1.17
Less distributions:					
Dividends from net investment income	(.49)	(.66)	(.73)	(.78)	(.72)
Net asset value, end of year	**$4.74**	**$5.24**	**$7.22**	**$7.45**	**$8.66**
Total return	**(.12%)**	**(19.14)%**	**7.16%**	**(5.13)%**	**14.97%**
Ratios/Supplemental Data:					
Net assets, end of year (in thousands)	$95,921	$116,924	$169,586	$174,805	$146,712
Ratio of expense to average net assets	1.23%(3)	1.04%(3)	.82%(3)	.81%(2)	.95%(2)
Ratio of net investment income to average net assets	9.72%(1)	10.61%	10.04%	9.81%	8.60%
Portfolio turnover rate	140%	184%	154%	140%	251%

(1) As required, effective February 1, 2001, the Fund has adopted the provisions of the AICPA Audit and Accounting Guide for Investment Companies and began amortizing premium on debt securities. The effect of this change for the year ended January 31, 2002 on net investment income and net realized and unrealized gains and losses was less than $.01 per share. The effect of this change was to decrease the ratio of net investment income to average net assets from 9.79% to 9.72%. Per share and ratios for the year prior to February 1, 2001 have not been restated to reflect this change in accounting policy.

(2) Before offset of custody credits.

(3) Ratio reflects expenses grossed up for custody credit arrangement. The ratio of expenses to average net assets net of custody credits would have been 1.24% for the year ended January 31, 2002 and would not have changed for the years ended January 31, 2001 and January 31, 2000.

Tip It is a mistake to choose a tax-exempt money market fund or tax-exempt bond fund unless justified by your federal and state tax rates. These funds are a poor choice for most individuals with modest amounts of taxable income.

The services offered and how these services operate The prospectus will explain whether the fund's sponsor offers features such as dividend reinvestment, check writing, and tax-sheltered retirement plans. Even though numerous funds may offer the same basic services, the fees they charge for these services may vary enough to influence your choice. For example, some funds charge a nominal fee for each check you write or for each switch of your money from one fund to another from the same sponsor. Likewise, some mutual fund sponsors are more lenient about allowing transfers from one fund to another. These differences may affect your decision to purchase shares of the fund.

8 Mutual Fund Alternatives

M utual funds are not the only type of investment that offers immediate diversification and professional selection of securities for individuals who have modest amounts of money to invest. Closed-end investment companies invest in a portfolio of securities with capital raised from selling a limited number of ownership shares. Another alternative, the unit investment trust, acquires and maintains a static portfolio that does not require active portfolio management. A newer alternative is exchanged-traded funds, a hybrid that incorporates features of mutual funds and closed-end investment companies whose shares trade on a securities exchange.

Mutual funds offer diversification and professional management of securities portfolios—two desirable investment attributes that most individual investors have difficulty achieving by themselves. Like most investment vehicles, mutual funds also have a downside. For one thing, the funds charge ongoing operating and management fees that reduce the returns you earn as a shareholder. These charges are not unfair because mutual funds incur expenses that are associated with managing a large investment portfolio. On the other hand, management fees charged by some large funds produce revenues that far exceed the costs of operating these funds. Many mutual funds also levy sales or redemption charges that must be paid by investors who purchase or sell shares.

A mutual fund's unique organizational structure can result in its stockholders suffering financial penalties. Mutual funds continually accept new investors and redeem the shares from existing investors so that mutual fund portfolio managers must adjust their investment policies to account for monies that flow into or out of the funds. Successful funds sometimes sell so many new shares and grow so rapidly that the portfolio managers have a difficult time identifying appropriate uses for the monies. Thus, fast growth may penalize investment results.

Several alternative investment vehicles have been developed to help offset some of the disadvantages of mutual funds. These alternatives have their own disadvantages, but these may not be particularly important to some investors. In other words, you may find that the three mutual fund alternatives discussed in this chapter are a better fit for your own needs.

Closed-End Investment Companies

Closed-end investment companies (also called *closed-end funds*) are operated in much the same manner as mutual funds. These companies employ professional portfolio managers who assemble and oversee portfolios of securities for the benefit of the firm's shareholders. The investment companies earn dividend and interest income that they distribute to their shareholders, who are required to report and pay taxes on the distributions. Closed-end investment companies also distribute capital gains realized from the sale of securities sold from their portfolios. These funds levy an ongoing charge to pay for the costs of operating the company and managing the fund's portfolio. To this point, the description of a closed-end investment company makes it seem identical to mutual funds.

The Organization of Closed-End Funds

The major difference between closed-end investment companies and mutual funds is the limited number of shares issued by closed-end funds. These firms raise capital by issuing a limited number of shares specified in their corporate charter. Additional shares of a closed-end fund are not continuously offered for sale and, in fact, are unlikely ever to be offered. Likewise, closed-end funds do not stand ready to redeem outstanding shares whenever stockholders decide that they would like to liquidate their investment. Closed-end investment companies are organized in an identical manner to most other corporations that have publicly traded common stock. The company initially issues a limited number of shares and may later sell additional shares, but only with the approval of the firm's existing shareholders. Closed-end investment company shares that are distributed as part of a new issue are expected by the fund's management and by investors to remain outstanding indefinitely (i.e., no redemptions will occur). As illustrated in Figure 23, closed-end funds are mostly marketed to investors interested in the high current income offered by bonds. At the end of 2002 assets held by closed-end bond funds amounted to nearly four times the value of assets held by closed-end equity funds.

Suppose a new closed-end investment company is formed

Figure 23 ■ Types of Assets Held by Closed-End Funds, Late 2002, in Billions of Dollars

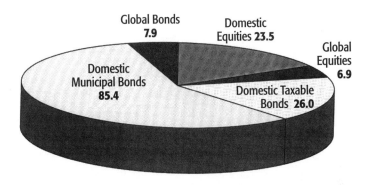

with an investment objective of earning high current income for its shareholders. The fund's portfolio managers intend to accomplish the objective by investing shareholders' money in long-term corporate bonds of low to medium credit quality. The fund's sponsor utilizes the services of an investment banking firm that solicits investors to purchase 20 million shares of the fund's stock at $10 per share in an initial public offering. The portfolio manager will have somewhat less than $200 million to invest because a small portion of the money raised from investors must be shared with the investment banker. For example, the investment banker may retain 30 cents for each share that is issued, causing the closed-end investment company to collect $9.70 for each share that is sold to investors for $10.

The types of bonds held in the fund's portfolio will determine the amount of interest income the fund will earn and the amount of dividends that will be distributed to shareholders. If interest rates are relatively high at the time the fund is organized, the portfolio manager will assemble a portfolio of high-coupon bonds that earn high interest income for the fund and enable the fund to pay hefty dividends to its shareholders. If interest rates are relatively low when the fund is formed, dividend payments to shareholders will be more modest. So long as the closed-end fund continues to hold the same bonds, the interest income it receives and the resulting dividend distributions to its shareholders will remain constant. Interest income will change only when issuers redeem bonds held in the fund's portfolio or the fund's portfolio managers choose to sell and replace bonds.

If market rates of interest subsequently decline following formation of the fund, the market values of all fixed-income securities including bonds held in the fund's portfolio will increase in value. Because the fund's sponsors decided to concentrate on owning bonds with long maturities, the fund's portfolio will gain substantially in market value as a result of reduced market interest rates. An increased portfolio value, in turn, is likely to cause an increase in the fund's net asset value and its share price. An increase in market interest rates would produce the opposite result with a fall in net asset value and share price.

Because no additional shares of stock are to be issued by the fund, portfolio managers will not be concerned about the need to invest large inflows of new money in low-coupon bonds (remember, interest rates have dropped) that would cause a reduction in the dividends paid to each of the fund's original shareholders. Likewise, closed-end funds do not stand ready to redeem outstanding shares so the fund's portfolio managers will not have to worry about selling bonds from the portfolio in order to raise money to pay for redeemed shares.

A closed-end investment company is managed as an ongoing firm that pays a portfolio manager to continually evaluate and adjust the fund's securities portfolio. The proceeds from the

> **Tip** Sponsors of closed-end investment companies claim their managers are better able to concentrate on achieving long-term performance goals because closed-end funds are not subject to share redemptions by unhappy shareholders. Mutual fund managers are more likely to concentrate on short-term performance.

sale of stocks or bonds from a fund's portfolio are reinvested in other stocks or bonds the portfolio managers consider more promising investments. For example, managers of an equity growth fund who expect a substantial decline in the stock market are likely to sell some of the fund's stocks or change the fund's portfolio to hold more conservative stocks. Bond fund managers who expect market rates of interest to increase are likely to decrease the average maturity length of the fund's bond portfolio in order to reduce losses that will result from falling bond prices.

How Closed-End Investment Fund Shares Are Valued

Closed-end investment company shares are actually accorded two values. Net asset value, the accounting value of an investment company's shares, is calculated in the same manner used to determine the NAV of a mutual fund's shares: the market value of the fund's portfolio less any debts divided by the fund's outstanding shares of stock. For example, a closed-end investment company holding securities with a market value of $18 million, no outstanding debt, and 1.2 million outstanding shares of stock has a net asset value of $18 million/1.2 million shares, or $15 per share. If the value of the fund's portfolio increases to $24 million, the new net asset value will be $24 million/1.2 million shares, or $20 per share. Only changes in the value of securities in the portfolio drive the net asset value of a closed-end fund.

Closed-end investment company shares are also valued according to the price at which the shares are traded among investors. The market value of a closed-end fund's shares may or may not equal the shares' net asset value. In the example just cited in which the fund's shares have a NAV of $15, the shares may trade among investors in the secondary market at a price of more than $15 or less than $15. A closed-end fund does not stand ready to redeem its own shares at net asset value, so shareholders who wish to sell their stock must locate other investors who are interested in buying the shares. There is no reason to believe that the price agreed to by the two parties will exactly equal the share's net asset value. Shares of closed-end investment companies are priced in the same manner as other stocks traded on the exchanges and in the over-the-counter market. That is, the price is established by the supply and demand from investors.

Why might the shares of a closed-end fund sell for more than net asset value? In other words, why would a closed-end fund be valued at more than the market value of its portfolio? Good question. Suppose an investment company's portfolio managers

---

Tip

Investment companies that invest in a single country or in emerging markets are generally organized as closed-end funds because management wants to limit the amount of funds that must be invested and also restrict redemptions. Equities held in these funds often lack the liquidity that is required to effectively manage an open-end fund that allows unlimited redemptions.

> **Tip**
>
> If you are considering the purchase of a closed-end fund that sells at a discount to NAV, check to determine how the current discount compares to the historic discount. A fund selling at a 10-percent discount from NAV may not be quite as good a bargain if the discount was previously much greater.

are able to consistently produce superior investment performance compared to other funds and compared to stock market averages. The fund has a record of paying good dividends and distributing capital gains at the same time the net asset value and share price rise. This performance is likely to result in the fund's stockholders being pleased with their investment. Outstanding performance typically garners substantial publicity, causing other investors to consider moving their money to the care of the fund's managers. The investors cannot buy shares directly from the fund (remember, a closed-end fund has a limit on the number of outstanding shares) and must place orders with brokerage firms who must rely on existing stockholders of the fund who might be interested in selling their shares. The current stockholders realize they hold a good investment and will be reluctant to part with their shares unless they receive a premium price. Even the best investments are for sale at some price. Investor demand occasioned by superior investment performance is likely to cause the shares of the closed-end investment company to trade at a price that is higher than the net asset value.

Now consider a closed-end fund that employs portfolio managers who have posted poor investment results for several years running. Current stockholders of the fund can only liquidate their shares by finding other investors who wish to buy. Other investors are likely to shun the fund unless its shares can be purchased at a discount from net asset value. The worse the fund's investment performance, the larger the discount investors are likely to demand in order to buy the shares. Why pay full price to buy into a closed-end fund that is managed by professionals who can't match the returns on a popular stock average?

How Shares of a Closed-End Fund are Traded

The shares of a closed-end investment company are traded by specialists on the organized exchanges and by securities dealers in the over-the-counter market. The shares of these funds are traded through dealers and specialists at whatever prices cause a balance of supply and demand. A dealer who experiences an excess of demand over supply in the shares of a closed-end fund (investors are entering more orders to buy than other investors are entering orders to sell) is likely to raise the bid price of the shares in order to attract more sellers and to raise the ask price in order to attract fewer buyers. The share price of a closed-end fund is influenced by orders to sell the shares and orders to buy the shares.

Buying or selling shares of a closed-end fund requires that you employ the services of a brokerage company with access to the markets in which the shares are traded. If the shares of a closed-end fund are primarily traded on the New York Stock Exchange, a brokerage company is likely to transmit an order for the fund's shares to the floor of the NYSE. Orders will be transmitted to the appropriate dealer when shares are traded in the over-the-counter market.

You can participate in a new offering of closed-end investment company shares by entering an order with a member of the syndicate that is bringing the issue to market or with a broker who will purchase shares in the investment company from a syndicate member. Closed-end funds with an investment objective compatible with your investment needs are relatively infrequent, and you are likely to end up buying shares from another investor in the secondary market. Because closed-end funds do not stand ready to redeem their shares, shareholders who wish to dispose of shares must locate other investors who are interested in purchasing the shares. This nearly always requires that the shareholders employ the services of a brokerage company that will be able to send the order to a market in which the stock is traded.

Although shares of a closed-end fund are sold without a sales fee, investors must pay a brokerage commission when shares are purchased and again when the same shares are sold. The size of the brokerage fee depends on the number of shares being bought or sold and the commission schedule of the brokerage firm you select to undertake the transaction. Some Internet-based brokerage firms will buy or sell up to 5,000 shares for a fee of $10 to $25. Full service brokerage firms that offer advice charge considerably more for the same transaction. The lack of a sales fee to buy shares in a closed-end fund stems from the fund's fixed number of shares. Once the shares have been distributed there is no reason to advertise or employ salespersons in an attempt to attract additional investors.

Unit Investment Trusts

Unit investment trusts (UITs), also called *unit trusts* and *investment trusts*, are another investment vehicle that offers both immediate diversification and professional selection of securities. UITs are particularly popular with investors who seek tax-exempt income through municipal bond ownership. Municipal bonds are normally issued and traded in minimum denominations of $5,000, an amount too large for many individual investors, especially if the investors have an interest in holding a diversified bond portfolio.

The sponsor of an investment trust assembles a portfolio of securities and sells pieces, or "units," of the trust to investors. Income earned by the trust is passed along to owners of the trust's units. A trust's owners each receive periodic income payments from the trust in proportion to the number of units they hold. For example, the owner of ten units of a unit trust will receive double the payments received by an investor owning five units of the same UIT. To this point, the description of the unit investment trust makes it appear virtually identical to a mutual fund or a closed-end investment company.

A major difference between UITs and investment companies is the extent to which the securities portfolio of an investment trust is managed—it isn't! Mutual funds and closed-end investment companies pay hefty compensation to professional portfolio managers who are expected to use their expertise to trade securities and improve shareholders' returns. The portfolio of a unit investment trust does not require continuous management because no trading occurs once the portfolio is assembled. Rather, the portfolio, once assembled, is left alone and continuous management expertise is not required.

How a Unit Trust is Organized

Suppose a financial services company decides to offer investors partial ownership in a diversified portfolio of municipal bonds. The firm knows that investors are always interested in earning tax-free income, a desire that is reinforced by the likelihood that federal income tax rates may soon be increasing. The firm purchases approximately $10 million each of 15 different municipal bond issues for a total investment of $150 million.

The bonds are acquired in the secondary market from other institutional investors.

Units of the trust will be sold to investors at a price equal to the total market value of the bonds held in the trust divided by the number of units being sold. For example, if the sponsors decide to organize the trust with 150,000 ownership units, each unit will be sold to investors for approximately $1,000 ($150 million/150,000 units). Units of the trust are sold through sales agents who charge a fee for their service.

The rate at which new trusts are formed depends upon investors' demand for this particular type of investment product. If investors have recently exhibited an interest in high-yield, high-risk junk bonds, sponsors will organize and market new trusts that hold portfolios of these securities. When one trust has been successfully distributed, the sponsor is likely to begin the process yet again, assuming there is sufficient investor demand. If investors enter a period in which they are concerned about the risks of investing in securities, sponsors are likely to concentrate on organizing new trusts that own portfolios of U.S. government securities or high-grade corporate bonds. Sponsors often organize trusts with portfolios that have a narrow focus. Some trusts concentrate on investments in a particular region of the world, or a certain state or region in the United States. For example, unit trusts that own tax-exempt municipal bonds issued in the state of New York are very popular because of the high tax rates faced by residents of that state and the large number of New York residents who are potential customers. Investment trusts holding portfolios of tax-exempt bonds issued in California are also very popular.

Unlike mutual funds and closed-end investment companies that maintain actively managed portfolios, the sponsor of a unit investment trust oversees the portfolio but does not trade or

> **Tip** Unit trusts are a particularly appropriate investment choice when you find it desirable to receive a periodic return of principal as well as interest income. Unit trusts slowly liquidate as principal from redeemed bonds is passed through to the trusts' owners.

manage the securities held in the portfolio. Basically, the securities that comprise the trust's portfolio at the time the units are first distributed to investors are the securities that will comprise the portfolio throughout its life. In the case of the municipal bond trust discussed earlier in this chapter, the same municipal bonds will be held until redeemed by their issuers. Some bonds may be redeemed early while other bonds will be held in the portfolio until the scheduled maturity. At some point all the bonds that were acquired when the unit trust was formed will be redeemed.

Bonds deemed overvalued are not sold from the trust's portfolio and immediately replaced by other bonds with higher yields, superior risk characteristics, or different maturities. Likewise, the money received from any bond redemptions will be passed along to the owners of the trust rather than reinvested in additional bonds. Investors who purchase units of an investment trust that holds a portfolio of bonds will have their original investment gradually returned at the same time they are receiving income from interest payments received by the fund and passed through to owners. Annual interest income earned by the trust and distributed to the trust's owners will decline over time as bonds held by the trust mature.

The schedule by which the bonds in a trust's portfolio will mature or the extent to which the securities will be redeemed early depends upon the particular types of bonds a sponsor has selected. Some trusts are organized with portfolios of relatively short-term bonds that mature in five years or less. Other trusts specialize in owning intermediate-length or long-term bonds that are likely to pay interest for many years.

The Value of a Unit Investment Trust

The value of a trust unit depends upon two variables: the value of the assets held in the trust's portfolio and the number of outstanding ownership units of the trust. An investment trust that holds a portfolio with a market value of $100 million and has 100,000 outstanding ownership units will have its units valued at approximately $1,000 each. If the market value of the trust's portfolio increases, there will be a proportionate increase in the value of each of the ownership units. For example, the units of an investment trust that holds a portfolio of long-term bonds will increase in value if market rates of interest decline. The more that interest rates decline, the more the market value of the trust's portfolio and the trust's units of ownership will increase. The investment success of a unit investment trust depends not upon the trading skills of portfolio managers, but rather upon the securities that are initially selected to comprise the trust portfolio.

If you purchase units of a trust during the original distribution,

Tip Although the sponsors generally make a secondary market in their own unit trusts, you should generally plan on holding a unit trust until all of the assets are liquidated. Selling units in the secondary market is likely to mean you will be penalized on the price you receive because the secondary market for these investments is relatively illiquid.

you are reasonably assured of having all or most of your outlay eventually returned so long as the trust holds secure investments and so long as you hold the units until the trust is eventually dissolved. However, if you purchase a unit investment trust after the original distribution date, you could receive more or less than you pay because trust ownership units are subject to changing values as securities that comprise the portfolio change in value.

Most sponsors of unit investment trusts maintain a secondary market in units of the trusts they originate. The secondary market allows you to sell investment trust units that you have purchased but no longer wish to own. Selling back to the sponsor means you are likely to receive a price based on the bid prices of bonds held in the portfolio. You may also purchase previously issued UITs in the secondary market.

Expenses Involved in Investing in Unit Investment Trusts

UITs don't require a lot of management, but they do often require a substantial amount of selling effort. The main cost of investing in a unit investment trust is the 2 percent to 5 percent purchase cost. The sales fee is a one-time charge paid at the time units are purchased. For example, if you invest $10,000 in a unit investment trust that charges a 5 percent sales fee, you will be charged a commission of $500 in addition to the $10,000 principal amount of the purchase.

Sponsors of unit trusts typically establish commission schedules with sliding fees that depend on the amount of money invested. The sponsor of a trust may charge a commission of 4.5 percent for purchases of up to 200 units, 4 percent for purchases of 201 to 400 units, and so forth. Trust units purchased in the secondary market (as opposed to units purchased when a trust is initially formed) also carry a sales commission determined by a schedule that may differ somewhat from the com-

Figure 24 ■ Typical Sales Fees for a Municipal Bond Unit Trust

	Sales Charge as a Percentage of Offering Price	
Number of Units	Initial Offering	Secondary Market
less than 250	4.5%	5.5%
250 to 499	3.5	4.5
500 to 749	3.0	3.5
750 to 999	2.5	2.5
1,000 or more	2.0	2.0

mission originally charged on the same units. The sponsor that resells trust units will have purchased these units from another investor. A trust sponsor attempts to profit from secondary transactions by selling the units at a slightly higher price than it pays to purchase the units and also by charging a sales fee. Figure 24 illustrates typical sales fees charged to investors who purchase a unit investment trust.

Exchange-Traded Funds

In 1993 the American Stock Exchange commenced trading a new product, the exchange-traded fund (ETF), which has since grown both in variety and importance. An exchange-traded fund is a mutual fund that trades on a securities exchange in the same manner as the shares of General Motors, Procter & Gamble, AT&T, or any other common or preferred stock. Investor orders are transmitted to the floor of an exchange where a specialist matches an order to sell with an order to buy. When orders can't be matched the specialist will buy shares for and sell shares from her own account. In other words, shares of an

ETF are not purchased from or sold back to the fund's sponsor as is the case with regular mutual funds. Rather, shares of an exchange-traded fund are bought or sold by entering an order with a broker who transmits your order to the floor of an exchange. Exchange-traded funds offer the same major advantage as a regular mutual fund—the ability to acquire an ownership stake in hundreds of different stocks with a single purchase.

How Exchange-Traded Funds are Organized

ETFs are organized in an unusual manner that is a cross between a mutual fund and a closed-end investment company. An exchange-traded fund assembles a portfolio so as to track the investment performance of a particular stock market index such as the Standard & Poor's 500 Index or the Dow Jones Industrial Average (DJIA). This task is accomplished by acquiring the same stocks in the same proportions used in calculating the index it is designed to track. For example, one exchange-traded fund, popularly called *Diamonds* because of its DIA ticker symbol, is comprised of the 30 stocks utilized in calculating the Dow Jones Industrial Average. The share price of this fund tracks the market value of the DJIA. Shares of another popular ETF track the performance of the Standard & Poor's 500 Index. These shares are called *Spiders* (actually, SPDR) after the acronym for Standard & Poor's Depository Receipts. The most popular ETF goes by the name *Cubes* because of its QQQ ticker symbol. This ETF is constructed to track the performance of the Nasdaq 100. To this extent ETFs are no different from regular index funds, mutual funds that pursue the goal of tracking the market performance of a particular index. For example, one of America's largest mutual funds, the Vanguard 500 Index Fund, is assembled to track the performance of the Standard & Poor's 500 Index.

ETF shares traded in the secondary market represent partial ownership of a securities portfolio assembled by a sponsor. In this respect, ETFs are like closed-end investment companies. However, while shares of a closed-end investment company can trade at a significant premium or discount to the value of the underlying portfolio, ETFs are constructed to trade at very close to net asset value. When ETFs are formed, rather than issue shares to the public, the sponsor exchanges large blocks of ETF shares called *creation units* for securities that will comprise the trust portfolio. The securities comprise the underlying index the ETF is established to track. Broker-dealers then break the creation units into shares that are offered to investors. These are the ETF shares that trade on exchanges.

Changes in investor demand cause creation units to be continually created and redeemed. Shares of an ETF closely track the value of the portfolio because large investors are permitted to exchange creation units for the appropriate basket of securities or trade the appropriate basket of securities for additional creation units. A disparity between the value of ETF shares and the underlying basket of securities that represent the index will result in arbitrage by broker-dealers until the disparity in values is eliminated. For example, if the value of the underlying securities is higher than the price of the ETF, institutional investors will exchange creation units to the sponsor in return for the underlying securities.

Comparing ETFs with Mutual Funds

Although exchange-traded funds provide investment performance that is similar to mutual funds, the two types of investments have some important and some not so important differences. These include:

1. Share prices for exchange-traded funds are updated continuously while mutual fund shares are priced at the end of the trading day.

2. ETFs generally have very low expense ratios, even compared to index funds that tend to have much lower expense ratios than the typical equity fund. This can be a significant advantage for investors who anticipate long holding periods.

3. Unlike mutual funds, orders to buy or sell exchange-traded funds can specify a price limit. For example, you can instruct your broker to purchase shares of an ETF only if the price drops to a certain level. Likewise, you can specify a minimum price you will accept to sell shares of an ETF.

4. Exchange-traded funds can be sold short. That is, you can borrow and sell shares of an ETF in anticipation that the price will decline. This is an important issue only if you sometimes sell short to bet on a market decline or hedge another investment position. Most individual investors do not engage in short selling.

5. Unlike mutual funds, ETFs can be purchased on margin. In other words, you can use borrowed money to increase your stake in an ETF. The ability to purchase on margin adds flexibility but will cause bigger losses in the event the ETF you buy subsequently falls in value.

6. Buying and owning ETF shares does not entail a sales charge, redemption fee, or 12b–1 fee, but you will pay a brokerage commission both to buy and to sell these shares. The commission you pay will depend on the brokerage firm you utilize. Some Internet brokers charge as little as $5 to buy or sell 1,000 shares.

9 Sources of Information about Mutual Funds

There has been an explosion in recent years of financial and investment information of all kinds including reporting on mutual funds. Most people have a limited amount of time to devote to this information and so it is important to be able to select the most useful sources. Mutual fund price quotations are available on a daily and weekly basis in many widely available publications. Information on specific mutual funds is offered by several popular periodicals and a number of specialized publications. The Internet has become an excellent source of current information on prices and performance along with commentary about mutual funds.

You are most likely to select investments appropriate to your needs when you are an informed investor. To become informed you must know where to obtain specific kinds of investment information. Suppose you are watching a television discussion about investments and several of the participants mention that they believe it is a good time to invest in the petroleum industry. The analysts forecast an increasing demand for petroleum-based products and a resulting increase in petroleum prices and higher profits for companies in the industry. You have evaluated your own investment goals and determined that an investment in the petroleum industry is an appropriate fit with the other investments you currently own. Rather than purchase shares in a single company, you would like to buy into the portfolio of a mutual fund that holds a diversified portfolio of petroleum stocks. Do any mutual funds specialize in investments in this industry? If so, how can you obtain information about their fees, expenses, and investment track records?

Perhaps you have decided that you would like to increase your current investment income by acquiring shares in a mutual fund that invests in long-term government securities. How can you determine which of these specialized funds have historically offered the highest yields and which funds invest only in direct obligations of the U.S. government? If you have decided to limit your selection to a no-load fund, how do you go about locating the addresses, phone numbers, or web addresses of sponsors that sell their funds directly to investors?

Information about Mutual Funds

The Investment Company Institute, the industry-sponsored association of mutual funds, closed-end investment companies, and unit investment trusts, makes available without charge several excellent publications including *Reading the Mutual Fund Prospectus*. The Institute also publishes a mutual fund directory that provides addresses, phone numbers, and information on minimum investment requirements and types of fees charged. The directory is available from the Institute for a nominal

---

Tip It is important to stay informed by reading a financial newspaper such as *The Wall Street Journal* or *Financial Times*. Informed investors tend to make better financial decisions.

charge. The Investment Company Institute may be reached at 1401 H Street, NW, Suite 1200, Washington, DC 30005 (202-293-7700), or via their website at http://www.ici.org.

Mutual fund share values are published daily in most large metropolitan newspapers. *The Wall Street Journal* includes an extensive daily listing of mutual fund share prices while most other papers have abbreviated listings both in terms of the number of funds included and the amount of data published for each listing. Mutual fund shareholders can obtain current mutual fund values by calling the appropriate fund, usually via a toll-free number. For those with access to the Internet, mutual fund sponsors generally provide a whole raft of information including pricing data. *Barron's*, a sister publication of *The Wall Street Journal* that is published each Monday, contains weekly price data that includes each fund's 52-week high and low prices. It also presents information about recent dividend and capital gains distributions.

Figure 25 (p. 144) illustrates mutual fund price listings as they often appear in daily newspapers. The Scott Group is shown as the sponsor of four funds. Entries in the NAV column indicate the net asset value for each fund at the close of trading on the previous trading day. In other words, Wednesday's trading data is published in Thursday's newspaper. Scott Government Bond Fund has a NAV of $10.30, an amount that is calculated by dividing the number of the fund's outstanding shares into the market value of the fund's portfolio of government bonds less any debts owed by the fund. This represents the price at which shares are redeemed by the fund and issued to new investors. Entries under NAV Chg represent the changes in each fund's net asset value that occurred between the close of trading on this day and the previous trading day. According to the information provided, both the Scott Government Bond

Figure 25 ■ Mutual Fund Price Listings

Fund	NAV	NAVChg
The Scott Group		
Scott GvmtB	10.30	+ .10
Scott Growth	9.95	− .05
Scott Income	12.20	.....
ScottValueFd	15.90	+ .30

Fund and the Scott Value Fund increased in value during the day's trading while the Scott Growth Fund declined in value. A series of dots or no entry in this column indicates that no change in value occurred between the two trading dates.

Price information for closed-end investment companies is also included in the daily stock quotations of most large daily newspapers. Closed-end price quotations are presented in an identical manner to quotations for other common stocks. Both the closing prices and the respective net changes are included in most listings. A paper with a more detailed listing will include the high price and low price at which shares traded during the most recent 52 weeks. Some newspapers present price quotations for closed-end funds in a special section. These listings sometimes include data both for the net asset value and the stock price of each fund. Price quotations in sections reserved for closed-end funds are frequently presented in a manner similar to that illustrated in Figure 26.

Previous chapters identified net asset value as an important measure of a mutual fund's value. NAV is also of interest to investors in closed-end funds that generally sell at prices different from their respective net asset values. Some investors search

Figure 26 ■ Price Quotations for Closed-End Investment Companies

Fund	Exchange	NAV	Price	% Diff.
Mouseketeer Gvmt Bd	NYSE	13.35	13.75	+ 3.00
Vertigo Income Fd	NYSE	11.14	10.50	− 5.75

for closed-end investment companies that sell at big discounts to their net asset values. Figure 26 indicates the Mouseketeer Government Bond Fund had a closing price the previous trading day of $13.75 per share and that the shares carried a net asset value of $13.35. Thus, the shares currently sell at a 3 percent premium (represented by +) to net asset value. The percentage premium is calculated by dividing the difference between the two values by the NAV. The listing for Vertigo Income Fund indicates that the fund's shares closed at a price of $10.50, a 5.75 percent discount from the fund's net asset value.

Information about Individual Mutual Funds

Information about particular investment companies, including their fees, is available from a wide variety of sources including the funds themselves. Mutual funds have become such a popular investment that any publication dealing with personal investing will generally contain at least modest coverage of mutual funds. Several popular periodicals publish occasional issues that are almost exclusively devoted to mutual funds.

Information from Mutual Funds

Mutual fund sponsors and sales representatives are accustomed to bombarding the public with information regarding their products. Likewise, the sponsors expect huge numbers of requests for information. A sponsor of several different funds will normally offer a summary brochure that briefly describes each of the funds. Once you determine the type of mutual fund you are interested in owning (e.g., growth fund, income fund, or specialized sector fund), don't be bashful about calling or writing numerous sponsors and requesting a prospectus. It is often easier to visit the sponsor's website and view the material online. The mutual fund prospectus is one of the most informative circulars available from any source. Keep in mind when reading promotional information from a mutual fund sponsor that the firm is attempting to convince you to invest in the funds that it oversees.

Information from Periodicals

General business periodicals frequently publish articles and financial data about mutual funds. Some periodicals distribute special issues that include data on the short-term and long-term annual returns produced by individual funds. These special editions also generally include data on sales charges and annual expense ratios. *Business Week, Consumer Reports, Forbes, Money, Kiplinger's Personal Finance,* and *Worth* each offer special editions that present historical data for a large number of mutual funds. These and other publications often include some type of ranking system for mutual funds with similar investment objectives. For example, growth funds may be compared with one another in terms of their fees and historical returns. Publications also sometimes include an "honor roll" or "distinguished group" of funds that have consistently earned unusually high returns for their shareholders. The publications typically include a telephone number for each fund that is reviewed.

Popular periodicals are a good source for identifying specific funds in which you may want to invest. For example, if you have

> **Tip** Several popular money management magazines provide readers with mutual fund statistics and recommendations. While these recommendations are useful, you shouldn't rely on a single source of information in choosing a fund.

decided to invest in a mutual fund that has capital appreciation as an investment objective, use a listing supplied by one of the periodicals to identify a dozen or so funds that you find interesting from the standpoint of historical returns and reasonable fees. At this point you will want to obtain more detailed information about the funds in question. One source of detailed information is the prospectus that is available from each fund. These are available by mail or via the sponsor's website. Advisory services also provide information for a fee.

Mutual Fund Advisory Services

Many advisory and financial information services sell financial data and advice about individual mutual funds. Both the quality and the quantity of the information these firms provide vary substantially. Some advisory firms mail monthly newsletters, provide access to their website, or offer a publication plus access to a telephone "hotline" service. Subscription prices vary as widely as quality, so you should always request a sample before subscribing.

Value Line Publishing, a firm that is best known for *The Value Line Investment Survey*, publishes the biweekly *Value Line Mutual Fund Survey,* which analyzes 2,000 bond and equity funds. Using a format that is nearly identical to the older *Investment Survey*, Value Line provides information on each fund's portfolio holdings, management style, historical performance, and expenses.

Figure 27 ■ Sample Page from *The Value Line Mutual Fund Survey*

A 15-year performance graph is provided along with data on dividends, capital gains, portfolio turnover, and total return. The service also ranks each fund on a scale of one to five according to the fund's risk and historical return. Figure 27 illustrates a page from *The Value Line Mutual Fund Survey*.

Morningstar is probably the best-known purveyor of comprehensive information about mutual funds. This firm issues a biweekly publication that includes one page of descriptive information and financial data for approximately 120 different funds. A total of 10 different volumes are published during each 20-week period (i.e., 1 volume every other week for 20 weeks), at which point the cycle is repeated. Each biweekly mailing includes an index of all 1,240 funds covered by the service. The write-up for each fund includes information about historical performance, fees, the fund's largest portfolio holdings, a short descriptive analysis, and various services offered by the fund. Morningstar rates each mutual fund on the basis of the fund's risk-adjusted return. Figure 28 (p. 150) illustrates a page from the Morningstar service.

Numerous advisory services publish weekly or monthly newsletters for mutual fund investors. The services generally provide information on fees and historical returns for selected funds along with recommendations on which funds to buy and which funds to sell. If you are interested in sampling some of the services, pick up a copy of *Barron's* or another popular publication that contains a large number of advertisements from advisory services. You are also likely to come across advertisements from these services while surfing investment related sites on the Internet. Advisory services are generally willing to send sample copies on request.

Figure 28 ■ Sample Page from *Morningstar Mutual Fund Advisory Service*

Data through January 31, 2003

Vanguard 500 Index

Ticker	Load	NAV	Yield	Total Assets	Mstar Category
VFINX	None	$79.02	1.7%	$72,347 mil	Large Blend

Manager Strategy

The core of the fund's strategy is simple: Manager Gus Sauter buys and holds the stocks that compose the S&P 500 Index. Sauter attempts to add value on the margins by opportunistically buying futures contracts, among other techniques, and he actively tries to reduce trading costs.

Historical Profile

Return: Above Avg
Risk: Average
Rating: ★★★★ Above Avg

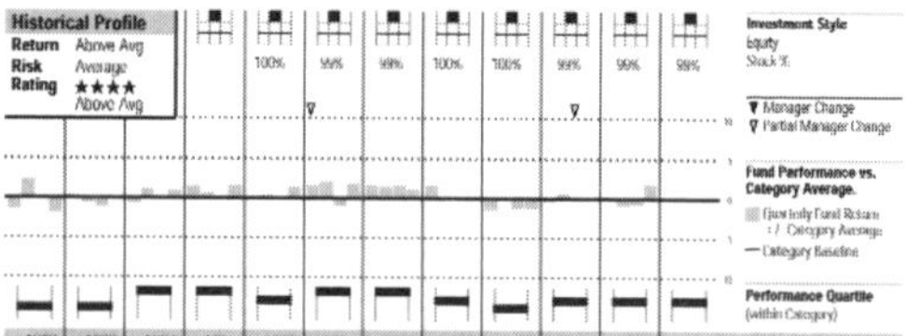

Portfolio Manager(s)

George U. Sauter. Since 10-87. AB'76 Dartmouth C.; MBA'80 U. of Chicago. Other funds currently managed: Vanguard Explorer Adm, Vanguard Mid Capitalization Index Adm, Vanguard Reit Index Adm.

1992	1993	1994	1995	1996	1997	1998	1999	2000	2001	2002	01-03	History
40.97	43.83	42.97	57.60	69.17	90.07	113.95	135.33	121.86	105.89	81.15	79.02	NAV
7.42	9.89	1.18	37.45	22.88	33.19	28.62	21.07	-9.06	-12.02	-22.15	-2.62	Total Return %
-0.20	-0.17	-0.13	-0.08	-0.06	-0.16	0.04	0.03	0.04	-0.14	-0.06	-0.01	+/-S&P 500
-1.62	-0.26	0.79	-0.32	0.43	0.35	1.60	0.15	-1.27	0.43	-0.50	-0.20	+/-Russ 1000
2.88	2.79	2.70	2.86	2.24	1.92	1.49	1.25	0.96	1.05	1.29	0.00	Income Return %
4.54	7.10	-1.52	34.59	20.64	31.27	27.13	19.82	-10.02	-13.07	-23.44	-2.62	Capital Return %
51	52	24	12	27	16	17	38	60	41	39	50	Total Rtn % Rank Cat
1.12	1.13	1.17	1.22	1.28	1.32	1.33	1.41	1.30	1.28	1.36	0.00	Income $
0.10	0.03	0.20	0.13	0.25	0.59	0.42	1.00	0.00	0.00	0.00	0.00	Capital Gains $
0.19	0.19	0.19	0.20	0.20	0.19	0.18	0.18	0.18	0.18	—	—	Expense Ratio %
2.81	2.65	2.72	2.38	2.04	1.66	1.35	1.13	0.98	1.14			Income Ratio %
4	6	6	4	5	5	6	6	9	4	....	....	Turnover Rate %
6,518	8,273	9,356	17,372	30,332	49,358	74,229	104,652	90,486	73,151	59,672	....	Net Assets $mil

Performance 01-31-03

	1st Qtr	2nd Qtr	3rd Qtr	4th Qtr	Total
1998	13.91	3.29	-9.95	21.39	28.62
1999	4.98	7.00	-6.25	14.96	21.07
2000	2.25	-2.62	-0.93	-7.81	-9.06
2001	-11.90	5.82	-14.72	10.65	-12.02
2002	0.24	-13.43	-17.22	8.39	-22.15

Trailing	Total Return%	+/- S&P 500	+/- Russ 1000	%Rank All Cat	Growth of $10,000
3 Mo	-2.98	-0.04	-0.42	74 40	9,702
6 Mo	5.32	0.06	0.02	63 32	9,468
1 Yr	-23.06	0.05	-0.49	73 42	7,695
3 Yr Avg	-13.88	-0.05	-0.22	71 49	6,387
5 Yr Avg	-1.35	-0.03	-0.14	68 35	9,341
10 Yr Avg	8.89	0.07	0.06	14 19	23,434
15 Yr Avg	10.84	-0.13	-0.15	15 22	46,819

Tax Analysis	Tax-Adj Rtn%	%Rank Cat	Tax-Cost Rat	%Rank Cat
3 Yr Avg	-14.30	41	0.50	21
5 Yr Avg	-1.88	26	0.54	21
10 Yr Avg	8.06	9	0.76	11

Potential Capital Gain Exposure: -2% of assets

Rating and Risk

Time Period	Load-Adj Return %	Morningstar Rtn vs Cat	Morningstar Risk vs Cat	Morningstar Risk-Adj Rating
1 Yr	-23.06			
3 Yr	-13.88	Avg	Avg	★★★
5 Yr	-1.35	Avg	Avg	★★★
10 Yr	8.89	+Avg	Avg	★★★★
Incept	11.73			

Other Measures	Standard Index S&P 500	Best Fit Index S&P 500
Alpha	0.1	0.1
Beta	1.00	1.00
R-Squared	100	100
Standard Deviation	16.45	
Mean	-13.88	
Sharpe Ratio	-1.11	

Portfolio Analysis 09-30-02

Share change since 06-02 Total Stocks: 498	Sector	PE	YTD Ret%	% Assets
General Elec	Ind Mtrls	15.4	6.00	3.24
Microsoft	Software	28.3	8.28	3.13
Wal-Mart Stores	Consumer	27.6	-7.36	2.90
ExxonMobil	Energy	23.7	-3.15	2.85
Pfizer	Health	23.4	-2.10	2.37
Johnson & Johnson	Health	26.0	2.96	2.13
Citigroup	Financial	10.7	5.25	1.98
American Intl Grp	Financial	20.4	16.68	1.89
Coca-Cola	Goods	30.9	-8.92	1.57
Procter & Gamble	Goods	25.6	-0.79	1.54
Merck	Health	17.8	-3.89	1.36
IBM	Hardware	28.0	0.01	1.31
Bank of America	Financial	12.9	1.65	1.27
Intel	Hardware	41.3	1.09	1.22
Philip Morris	Goods	7.1	-7.40	1.08
Wells Fargo	Financial	15.9	-1.51	1.08
Cisco Sys	Hardware	36.1	1.08	1.01
Verizon Comms	Telecom	—	-0.96	0.99
ChevronTexaco	Energy	—	-2.75	0.98
Viacom Cl A	Media		4.61	0.95

Current Investment Style

Market Cap %	
Giant	47.9
Large	37.1
Mid	14.5
Small	0.5
Micro	0.0
Median $mil:	41,574

Value Measures		Rel S&P 500
Price/Earnings	16.3	1.0
Price/Book	2.2	1.0
Price/Sales	1.0	0.9
Price/Cash Flow	5.5	1.0
Dividend Yield %	2.0	1.1

Growth Measures	%	Rel S&P 500
Long-Term Erngs	15.4	1.0
Book Value	8.1	1.0
Sales	8.9	1.0
Cash Flow	7.6	0.9
Historical Erngs	6.8	1.1

Profitability	%	Rel S&P 500
Return on Equity	17.1	1.0
Return on Assets	8.6	1.0
Net Margin	9.0	1.0

Sector Weightings	% of Stocks	Rel S&P 500	3 Year High	3 Year Low
Info	19.5	0.9	30	19
Software	4.4	0.9	5	4
Hardware	7.8	0.8	16	8
Media	3.6	0.9	4	4
Telecom	3.6	0.9	5	4
Service	49.6	1.0	50	41
Health	15.3	1.0	15	14
Consumer	9.4	1.1	9	7
Business	4.1	1.0	4	3
Financial	20.8	1.0	21	17
Mfg	30.9	1.1	33	28
Goods	11.3	1.2	11	8
Ind Mtrls	11.0	1.0	12	11
Energy	5.8	0.9	7	6
Utilities	2.8	1.0	3	3

Composition

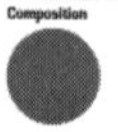

Cash	0.6
Stocks	99.3
Bonds	0.0
Other	0.1
Foreign (% of Stock)	0.1

Morningstar's Take by William Harding 01-29-03

Vanguard 500 Index has been bruised, but the thesis for owning it remains strongly intact.

Last year, many portfolio managers made the claim that it was a stock-picker's market, and their ability to uncover the market's few winners or avoid the biggest losers would add value to returns. So how did the stock-pickers fare? About as well as this passively managed fund. This offering's 22.1% loss in 2002 was certainly poor, but it was right in-line with the return posted by the average actively managed large-blend fund.

Further, though the fund's lack of a cash cushion provides a head wind when stocks sink, it hasn't been catastrophic amid the market's swoon. The fund's 14.2% annualized decline for the trailing three years through Jan. 27, 2003, lands right around its category's midpoint. But that average showing may be a disappointment for investors who grew accustomed to the fund's peer-busting ways during the bull market.

That brings us to a potential criticism of this fund that has merit. Because the fund tracks the market-capitalization-weighted S&P 500 Index, much of its fortunes are tied to how the largest companies that dominate the index fare. When these mega-cap names led the way in the late 1990s, the index was extremely tough to beat. But that yardstick hasn't been quite as daunting in recent years as smaller firms have generally outpaced their larger counterparts.

Instead of trying to predict what size stocks will lead the market's next charge, investors should keep the big picture in mind. This fund's rock-bottom expenses, broad diversification, and manager Gus Sauter's ability to keep the fund's returns on top of those of the index have resulted in an attractive long-term risk/return profile. We see no reason why that should change and think this fund is a wonderful choice to anchor one's portfolio. To offset the mega-cap bias, investors should consider pairing this offering with a small- or mid-cap option.

Address:	Vanguard Financial Ctr. P.O. Box 2600, Valley Forge, PA 19482, 800-662-7447	Minimum Purchase:	$3000	Add: $100	IRA: $1000
		Min Auto Inv Plan:	$3000	Add: $50	
		Sales Fees:	No-load		
Web Address:	www.vanguard.com	Management Fee:	0.18%		
Inception:	08-31-76	Actual Fees:	Mgt:0.16%	Dist: —	
Advisor:	Vanguard Core Management Group	Expense Projections:	3Yr:$58	5Yr:$101	10Yr:$230
Subadvisor:	None	Income Distrib:	Quarterly		
NTF Plans:	N/A	Total Cost (relative to category):	Low		

MORNINGSTAR® Mutual Funds

> **Tip** Rating stars awarded by Morningstar and Value Line serve as useful information but shouldn't be the only consideration in selecting a mutual fund. Make certain a fund's investment goals are compatible with your own goals. Purchasing shares of a highly-rated aggressive growth fund isn't a particularly good idea when you are seeking a conservative investment.

Information Via Your Computer

The Internet has become a mother lode for all types of investment information. The popularity and widespread ownership of mutual funds have resulted in many Internet sites devoting substantial space to information about these investments. Nearly all comprehensive business sites and most brokerage firm sites provide useful information about mutual funds. Here you can locate current mutual fund prices and, often, commentary on mutual funds. Internet sites of mutual fund companies provide pricing information for their own funds and generally allow online access to the prospectus for each of a sponsor's funds. It is less expensive for a mutual fund to provide online access to a prospectus than it is to send paper copies in the mail. Sites frequently include glossaries of terms that are relevant to mutual fund investing. In addition, some sites have excellent educational information regarding mutual funds. These sites typically provide information on the basics of mutual fund investing, including how to better understand the information in a prospectus and how to interpret a fee schedule. Some sites recommend and rank specific funds within investment objective categories. Much of this is information that was once only available for a fee.

The Internet has grown so rapidly and become so large that it is increasingly difficult and time-consuming to sort through all of the information that is presented. Even the most definitive search can turn up hundreds or even thousands of sites related to a particular topic. Sorting through all these sites is no easy task even for the most hardened web surfer. In addition, an Internet user always confronts the difficulty of determining whether the information being presented is accurate. Figure 29 includes the web addresses and a short description of the content for some of the better sites related to mutual fund investing. Figure 29 is by no means a comprehensive listing, but you should be able to locate most of the information you seek. Sites of mutual fund sponsors are omitted from the list because of biased information you may encounter. Still, sponsor sites often offer a variety of valuable information including basic educational material and guidance on choosing funds with appropriate investment objectives.

Figure 29 ■ Selected Internet Sites for Mutual Fund Investors

www.bloomberg.com/money/mutual
Commentary and current news relative to mutual funds
Top funds ranked by yield over one, two, and three years
Fund profiles including NAV, objective, historical returns, and related funds

www.fundsinteractive.com
Commentary and news relative to mutual funds
Links to mutual fund sponsors

http://cbs.marketwatch.com/pf/fund/
News and commentary on the mutual fund industry
Screening to compare funds on the basis of returns, risk, and fees

http://flagship.vanguard.com
Extensive educational material
Guidance on how to select a fund to meet your objectives
Planning tools for retirement

www.ici.org
Home page of the Investment Company Institute, an industry trade association
Educational material for mutual fund investors
Historical statistical information about the industry
Recent developments in the mutual fund industry
Explanation of industry regulations

www.kiplinger.com/investing/funds
Tips on how to select a fund
Information on how to get started in mutual funds
Includes a screening program to select mutual funds on the basis of criteria
    you enter

www.mfea.com
Excellent educational material on everything from reading a prospectus
    to understanding risk
Data on mutual fund NAVs, fees, and historical returns
News of the mutual fund industry

continued on next page

http://money.cnn.com/funds/
Fund screener to select mutual funds that meet specified attributes
Overview of returns and expenses for many funds
Commentary and news articles relevant to mutual funds

www.morningstar.com
Mutual fund news and commentary
Rankings of funds
Educational material relative to mutual fund investing
Extensive information on exchange-traded funds

www.sec.gov/answers/mutfund.htm
Excellent site with information about fees, rules, and types of funds
Includes a section on how to read a mutual fund prospectus
Tips on how to compare and evaluate different funds

www.smartmoney.com/funds/
News and commentary for mutual fund investors
Ranking of funds based on expenses, returns, etc.

Glossary

account fee A charge levied by some mutual funds for the maintenance of a shareholder account.

adviser An individual or organization that provides a mutual fund with investment advice.

asset allocation Distributing funds among several investments in some predetermined ratio.

automatic reinvestment Automatic purchases of additional shares of a mutual fund with dividends and/or capital gains distributions.

back-end load A sales fee paid by investors when mutual fund shares are redeemed. The fee is generally used by the fund to compensate brokers.

balanced fund A mutual fund with a portfolio that includes both bonds and stocks.

beat the averages To manage a portfolio so as to earn a return superior to the return calculated on stock market averages such as the Standard & Poor's Index.

bid The price offered for an asset.

bond rating The credit quality of a bond as judged by one of the major credit rating agencies.

break point The amount of money that must be invested in a mutual fund before the sales charge is reduced.

broker-dealer A firm that buys stock for and sells securities from its own portfolio and that also brings together buyers and sellers of securities.

buy-and-hold strategy The strategy of purchasing a security and holding it for a long period of time in the expectation that over the long term it will increase in value despite intervening swings in the market.

capital appreciation An increase in the net asset value of a mutual fund's shares.

capital gains distribution A payment of realized capital gains by an investment company to its shareholders.

check-writing privilege The privilege extended to a mutual fund shareholder of being able to write checks against the value of shares held by the investor. Shares of the fund are sold when the check is presented for payment.

classes Different types of shares issued by one fund. Each class holds the same investment portfolio and has the same investment objectives, but has different shareholder services and/or fees.

clone fund A mutual fund with a portfolio that is designed to emulate the portfolio of a different mutual fund.

closed-end investment company An investment company that issues a fixed number of authorized shares that trade in the secondary market among investors.

contingent deferred sales charge The fee levied by mutual funds on shareholder redemptions when shares have been held less than a specific length of time.

contractual plan A plan in which a mutual fund shareholder agrees to invest a predetermined amount of money in additional shares of the fund.

conversion Changing from one class of shares to another class of shares after a set period of time. A conversion generally allows a shareholder to enjoy lower annual expenses.

custodian An organization that retains custody of a mutual fund's assets.

direct marketing The sale of mutual fund shares directly to investors without the assistance of a salesperson.

discount brokerage firm A brokerage firm that discounts the commissions it charges customers to trade securities.

distribution fee See *12b–1 fee*.

diversification Purchasing assets that have returns that are not directly related. Diversification reduces the risk of investing.

dollar-cost averaging Investing equal amounts of money at periodic intervals.

double-exempt fund An investment company that invests in the bonds of a specific state and pays dividends that are exempt both from federal and state income taxes.

exchange fee A fee that some funds impose on shareholders who exchange shares of one fund to shares of another fund within the same fund group.

exchange-traded fund (ETF) A mutual fund whose shares trade on a securities exchange, generally at or very near net asset value per share.

ex-distribution Pertaining to mutual fund shares that trade without the right to a specific distribution.

ex-dividend Pertaining to mutual fund shares that trade without the right to a specific dividend.

expense ratio A mutual fund's total annual operating expenses (including distribution fees, management fees, and other expenses) expressed as a percentage of average net assets.

family of funds A group of mutual funds operated by the same sponsor.

front-end load A sales fee paid by investors when mutual funds are purchased. The fee is generally used by the fund to compensate the fund's sales agents.

fully invested Pertaining to a mutual fund that has used all of its cash balances to purchase securities.

fund switching Selling shares in one mutual fund and using the proceeds to purchase shares in a different mutual fund.

Ginnie Mae A wholly-owned government association that operates the mortgage-backed securities program designed to facilitate the flow of capital into the housing industry.

Ginnie Mae fund A mutual fund that invests in obligations guaranteed by Ginnie Mae and passes through to shareholders the interest and principal payments received by the fund.

growth fund A mutual fund that selects investments that are expected to increase in value.

high-yield bond A bond of low credit quality that subjects owners to substantial risk that interest and/or principal payments may not occur as scheduled. Also called *junk bond.*

income fund A mutual fund that selects investments that will provide current income to the fund's shareholders.

index fund A mutual fund that maintains a portfolio of securities designed to match the performance of the market or an identified segment of the market.

investment banker A company that assists organizations in raising money in the capital markets.

investment company A company that pools the funds of investors and purchases securities appropriate to the company's investment objectives.

Investment Company Institute (ICI) A national association for mutual funds, closed-end investment companies, and unit investment trusts. ICI collects and publishes industry data, represents its members in matters of regulation and taxation, and promotes the interests of the industry and its shareholders.

junk bond See *high-yield bond.*

liquidity A measure of an asset's or a portfolio of assets' ability to be easily converted into cash without affecting the market value.

load The fee charged to investors who purchase shares in a mutual fund. Also called *sales charge*.

low-load fund A mutual fund with a sales charge equal to 3 percent or less of the amount of money invested in shares of the fund.

management fee The payment of a mutual fund to its investment advisers. The management fee reduces the return of the fund's shareholders.

money market fund A mutual fund that holds a portfolio of high-quality short-term debt securities. These funds tend to offer great liquidity and safety at the expense of low returns.

Morningstar, Inc. A Chicago-based financial information service that is best known for its mutual fund publication and mutual fund rating system. The firm's star-based rating system is widely utilized by individual investors in selecting mutual funds.

municipal bond A debt issue of a city, county, state, or other political entity. Interest received from these securities is generally free of federal income taxes. Also called *muni*.

National Association of Securities Dealers (NASD) An organization of brokers and dealers that establishes legal and ethical standards for its members.

net asset value (NAV) The market value of a mutual fund's assets adjusted for debts and divided by the number of shares of the fund that are outstanding.

no-load fund A mutual fund that issues shares without a sales charge.

offering price The price at which a mutual fund's shares are issued to investors.

open-end investment company An investment company that continuously stands ready to redeem its own shares of stock. These firms are commonly referred to as mutual funds.

operating expenses The costs incurred by a fund including distribution fees, management fees, and other expenses.

over-the-counter market (OTC) A widespread web of dealers who make markets in many different securities.

portfolio A collection of assets.

portfolio manager An investment specialist who invests and manages a pool of assets.

portfolio turnover The degree to which a portfolio's assets are subject to trading activity. A high portfolio turnover tends to increase expenses and cause more taxable distributions to shareholders.

prospectus A legal document provided to investors by a firm that is distributing securities. A prospectus includes information that the investor will need in order to make an informed decision about whether or not to purchase the securities.

rating See *bond rating*.

rating agency A company that grades the credit quality of debt securities.

redemption fee A charge by some funds when shareholders redeem their shares. Redemption fees are paid to the fund, not a broker, and are generally limited to a maximum of 2 percent.

regulated investment company An investment company that meets federal regulations that allow it to escape taxation on dividends and realized capital gains that are passed through to the investment company's shareholders.

reinvestment privilege The privilege of a mutual fund's shareholders to automatically reinvest dividends and capital gains distributions in additional shares of the fund's stock.

sales charge See *load*.

sector fund A mutual fund that concentrates its portfolio holdings on securities of a restricted nature. For example, a sector fund may invest only in the securities of companies engaged in the health care industry.

Securities and Exchange Commission (SEC) The U.S. government agency established in 1934 and charged with protecting investors and maintaining the integrity of the securities markets.

tax-exempt money market fund A mutual fund that invests in short-term tax-exempt debt instruments and that pays federally tax-exempt dividends to shareholders.

total return With regard to mutual fund shares, the sum of returns earned from dividends, capital gains distributions, and change in share price.

transfer agent The organization that maintains records of a mutual fund's shareholders.

trustee A person or organization that manages the assets of some other person or organization.

turnover rate The number of shares traded by an investment company as a percentage of the firm's total portfolio.

12b–1 fee A fee paid from a mutual fund's assets in order to cover expenses for marketing and selling fund shares. These expenses might include advertising, broker compensation, and printing and mailing sales literature. Also called *distribution fee*.

unit investment trust An unmanaged portfolio of investments with ownership units that are sold to investors.

unrealized gain/loss The amount by which an owned asset's current value is greater or less than the asset's cost.

Value Line, Inc. A New York–based financial information company best known for its *Value Line Investment Survey*, a weekly analysis of approximately 1,300 stocks. Value Line also operates mutual funds, calculates and distributes a comprehensive stock index, and publishes the *Value Line Mutual Fund Survey*.

window dressing Changes in a mutual fund's portfolio in order to create the impression of successful investment choices. Mutual funds sometimes engage in window dressing prior to issuing a financial statement.

withdrawal plan An option of mutual funds that permits shareholders to sell shares in order to receive specified payments at regular intervals.

Index

About the Author

David L. Scott has taught finance and investing at the college and university level for over thirty years. During this period he has conducted workshops, written numerous articles, and authored nearly two dozen books on business finance, personal finance, and investing. He has been a guest on numerous radio shows and appeared on NBC's *Today* and on CNBC. Dr. Scott was born in Rushville, Indiana, and received degrees from Purdue University and Florida State University before earning a PhD in economics from the University of Arkansas.